MICHELLE KWAN

Heart of a Champion

an Autobiography

As told to Laura James

Scholastic Inc. / New York

This is for all the special people in my life who have encouraged me to aim high, work hard, and appreciate everything that I have. My deepest thanks to my parents, my grandparents, my sister Karen, my brother Ron, and my extended skating family for all their love and support both on and off the ice.

√S ℬT Lℰ

Unless otherwise credited, all photos courtesy of the Kwan family.
Flip art by David Mattingly

Library of Congress Cataloging-in-Publication Data Available

ISBN 0-590-76340-7

10 9 8 7 6 5 4 3 2 1

Printed in the U.S.A.

CONTENTS

Introduction

The first time I saw Michelle was in 1993 when she was twelve years old and skating in her first United States Figure Skating Championships. Even then she could do all the jumps the older skaters could do. She was very cute and showed great promise. Just two short years later that promise was realized when Michelle officially became the best skater in the world, winning the World Championships. She has become an artist of incredible depth, sensitivity, and maturity.

Michelle is a great athlete. But her extraordinary talent has not been the only key to her success. She has one of the best support teams the skating world has ever seen. Her parents, Danny and Estella; her coach, Frank Carroll; her choreographer, Lori Nichol; her sister Karen, a top-level skater herself; and her brother Ron form the core of a kind of *dream team* behind Michelle. They have pooled their wisdom and their love for her to give her their guidance in a fiercely competitive sport where the stakes get higher all the time.

In 1997 Michelle lost her national title before a stunned audience. We saw her fall, and we saw her tears afterwards. But a month later, Michelle was able to put her disappointment behind her and skate a beautiful program at the World Championships. Somehow she'd turned a painful experience into a lesson in love — love for her sport. Receiving her silver medal at Worlds, she looked every bit as happy as she had the year before when she had won the gold. I talked with Michelle a few minutes later backstage and she told me that the year had taught her some real tough lessons about skating and about herself, and that she was happy to skate well and regain her confidence again.

Now, with the Olympics approaching, her competitive drive seems unfazed. How could someone so young have such perspective? It's truly remarkable and a testament to Michelle's resilience and to the strength of her tight-knit family.

Danny and Estella Kwan have always encouraged their children to be their best, but they've never pushed them. They've always made skating Michelle's choice, not theirs. They've believed in her skating dreams with her, but they've carefully monitored the way in which those dreams interacted with her non-skating life. They've never let her lose her perspective on the sport.

Michelle enjoys life and she enjoys her sport. That joy just seems to spark out of her; it's been a big part of the pleasure I've taken in watching her grow over the years — as a young woman and as a skater. Through all of the ups and downs she's always had so much *fun*, and that's as it should be for someone her age. But she also has this remarkable level-headedness and perspective. Her priorities are always straight. And that is a truly incredible talent, one way beyond her years.

Peggy Fleming Jenkins

1
Falling Down

February 15, 1997: This was the date I'd been preparing for all season long, the date of the U.S. Figure Skating Championships in Nashville, Tennessee. I was backstage, just minutes before my long program, and something didn't feel right.

This was the fifth time I'd been to this major annual competition, but it was my first time skating as the defending national and world champion. Reporters had been saying that I looked unbeatable. But personally I didn't feel any more unbeatable that night than I did at my first Nationals, when I was a twelve-year-old kid with a ponytail, hoping to finish in the top ten. No one expected much from me then. Now everyone expected me to win.

My coach, Frank Carroll, was helping me to

get ready backstage. Together we tried to shut out all the noise around us so that we could concentrate. I closed my eyes, like I always do, and tried to see myself doing all four minutes of my long program. In a very, very short time it would all be over, and everyone would know if I really *was* unbeatable.

I knew something was wrong because I couldn't get this one picture out of my head: a picture of me, falling. "Go away," I'd say. But the image wouldn't leave. I wanted to be perfect, but backstage all I could think about were the things that could go wrong!

"No one can be perfect all the time," Frank said, trying to get me to stop worrying so much. "Don't defend, attack!"

It was time to skate. I glided onto the ice. The crowd cheered for me and then went silent. I reached one hand up to the ceiling and took my opening pose, like I'd done hundreds of times in practice. The music started, slowly, and I lunged forward. There was so much time to *think* between the beats of the music!

Have fun, Michelle, I told myself. It's just a sport.

Usually I'm so excited to be skating that I don't have to remind myself to have fun. But lately I'd felt the pressures of the sport more sharply. Just think about it: You work all year on your program, until you can do it in your sleep. You practice each jump thousands of times. And then it all comes down to four minutes on the ice! Your skating life can forever be changed by what happens during those four minutes.

Once the music picked up and I started skating faster, I felt better. I'd practiced the program so many times, I didn't have to think about what came next. I did my first two jumps, a triple-Lutz/double-toe combination, cleanly. The triple Lutz and I have never gotten along too well, and I was glad to get past it. But it was too soon to feel relieved.

The next combination was my hardest — a triple-toe/triple-toe combination. The first jump was clean, but I chickened out and made the second one a double instead of a triple.

But when I came down from the jump, my foot slipped from under me. I put a hand on the ice to catch myself, but it didn't do any good. The rest of my body followed, *thump*, on the ice. Just like the picture I couldn't shake!

The first thing you learn when you start to skate is how to fall. And the first thing you learn when you become a top-level skater is to get right back up. I automatically jumped to

my feet and continued my program. I flew
into a sit spin with a panicked look on my face.

Things kept getting worse. On a triple flip, I
landed badly and put my hand on the ice. I approached my next triple jump with far too
much doubt. I spun through the air, and just as
I landed, my whole body went down again.
There I was, flat on the ice, with the whole
world watching.

I didn't think I'd be able to pull myself together. But as I got up, I heard an amazing
sound. People were clapping in time to the
music. I was skating terribly, but the crowd
was cheering me on! I'd never had that
happen before. They were trying to give me
courage. And it worked. Their clapping woke
me up!

My next jump, a double Axel, was fine. I
backed off my next triple Lutz and only did a
double, but at least it was clean. And my last
two big jumps went well.

The music ended and I skated off the ice. All
I could think was, What have I done?! Tears
were streaming down my face. I couldn't stop
them. Frank put his arms around me to com-
fort me while we waited for my scores. But
when I saw them, I started crying all over
again.

I wasn't surprised by my scores. They only confirmed what had just taken place. Frank wasn't kidding when he said, "You can't always be perfect!"

"You'll skate another day," he said now, in a forgiving voice. Frank always knows the right thing to say. But he didn't have the answers to the questions that were racing through my mind: How could I have done that? Why did I panic? What could I do so that it would never happen again?

I was still crying when we went backstage. People from the TV network came to ask me to talk on air, but I couldn't yet. Frank asked them to give me a minute. But they kept coming back.

I knew that the people watching on TV wanted to know if I was okay. I knew that I owed them an answer. So I pulled myself together and went out to face the cameras. I did my best to explain what had happened, how I'd panicked, and how it felt to come in second place, but I didn't understand it myself yet.

How *did* it feel? I didn't know. I needed to talk to my family and figure out what had happened.

Later, after everyone had gone home and the arena was empty, my mom gave me a hug, which I really needed. Then my dad came to me and asked, "Well, Michelle, what did you learn from this?"

I now had an answer. "I learned that I need to love the sport again," I told him.

That was it, exactly. There's nothing I can do to ensure that I'll never have a bad night again. But, win or lose, I have to try not to forget why I'm on the ice in the first place: I love to skate. That's why I've been doing it all my life.

Skating is in my *heart*, not my head. From the time I was five, skating had always made me feel like I was flying. Just being on the ice made me happy. But at Nationals I was so busy trying not to fall that I forgot to feel what was in my heart.

I'd forgotten about my love of *skating*. And I guess you could say that love, which started back when I was still a pipsqueak eating candy and playing with stuffed animals, is what my story is all about.

2

The Kwan Family

I can't tell you about myself without telling you about my family first: my mother, Estella; my father, Danny; my sister, Karen; and my brother, Ron.

Our family has two top-level skaters: me and my sister, Karen, who is two years older than me. Karen finished seventh at the 1997 Nationals in Nashville. Ron likes to joke about "the famous Kwan sisters." He says nobody even knows we have a brother. But we do! We call him Ronald the Great. He's four years older than me, and if he didn't start playing ice hockey when I was five years old, Karen and I might never have gotten into skating.

With two figure skaters in the family, you might think that we inherited some special jumping and spinning gene from our parents or grandparents. But as far as I know, Karen and I are the first in our family even to dream of doing a triple toe loop.

My parents, Danny and Estella, were born in China. My mother was born in Hong Kong where she had a happy childhood and a big, loving family. She was an excellent student, and she loved music and ballet. When she was a teenager she was like I am now in lots of ways. That's probably why we get along so well!

She worked hard but also liked to have fun. And, like me, she never did anything without first thinking through all the consequences very carefully. It takes us both a long time to make decisions, even little ones.

My father was born in a little village near the Chinese city of Canton (now called Guangzhou). From what I've heard, life in China has changed and improved a lot since he was a kid. But back in the days of his childhood, life could be hard.

Dad's family had lived in Guangzhou for a long, long time. When my grandfather was born there were already lots of children in his family, and there wasn't enough food to go around. So his parents sent him to work for a rich farmer. For several years, from the time he was five, my grandfather spent his days and nights on that farm, watching over a single cow.

Later on he married my grandmother, and they started having kids. Then, a few years later, just two months before my father was born, Grandpa left the village, alone, to try to make a better life for his family someplace else.

Life was hard for my dad and his family. My dad tells about how he would get up at four o'clock in the morning to be the first in line to buy a small portion of meat. He didn't go to school or even meet his father until he was eight years old. But he learned a lot of lessons about life that school never could have taught him.

By the time my father was eight, my grand-father had moved to Hong Kong. Once he was settled, he sent for his family. My father started attending the school where my mother was also a student. Their families were friends, so they got to know each other.

Dad says he always had a little crush on Mom, but it was a long time before they fell in love. Anyway, I don't think they had much in common in those days: My mother was one of the best students, and my father, who had a lot of catching up to do, was near the bottom of the class.

My dad started working when he was thirteen years old. Even then he was ambitious, with big dreams for the future. He was a messenger for a few years, and later got a job working for the telephone company. He first came to America in 1971, when he was twenty-two, to attend a family wedding in California. He saw a chance to make the kind of life he'd always dreamed of, and he decided to stay.

He started out working in a restaurant, where he learned to cook. Then he also took a job with the telephone company in Los Angeles. Pretty soon, he and a partner opened up their own restaurant, the Golden Pheasant, in Torrance, which is just south of L.A. He worked very hard. He wanted to succeed.

Meanwhile, my mother was in Hong Kong, working as a nurse in a hospital. She loved taking care of people, but it was hard for her to watch them suffer. She needed a change, and (after thinking it over a lot) she made a big one — she became a television news anchorwoman!

That's what she was doing the next time she saw my father, when he came home to Hong Kong for their school reunion. And that's when they fell in love.

Soon they got married and moved back to the United States together. My mother, my father, and both of his parents lived in Torrance, and everybody helped out at the Golden Pheasant. Ron was born first, and then Karen came two years later.

My parents felt like they had a full house. "That's enough!" they said. "No more kids for now." They didn't want to see any of their kids suffering because there wasn't enough to go around.

But surprise! On July 7, 1980, I came into the world. My father named me Michelle, after his favorite song by his favorite band, the Beatles. It's a song about a boy who loves a girl, a beautiful girl with a beautiful name — Michelle.

We speak a mixture of Chinese and English at home. My father tells lots of stories about the old life in China. I always — even when I skate — wear a necklace that my grandmother gave me. It has a little Chinese dragon on it and a symbol that means good luck. Karen, Ron, and I are very close to our grandparents. Even though they don't speak much English, we understand one another.

I've been to China twice — once to skate, not long ago. The first time I was there was when I was very little and my mother took us to Hong Kong to meet her side of the family. I was too young then to remember much about that trip now, but Mom always says she's so glad she took us. Just a little while after we were there, her mother — my grandmother — died. It was so nice that she'd seen us and hugged us first.

But life in China still seems so far away from my life, and so different. Where did my competitive spirit come from? How did my parents end up with a daughter like me, who is so completely into one sport?

Actually, I can see similarities between what I do and what my parents did in coming to America. They wanted to start a family in a place where they could work hard and keep their kids happy and healthy. America was a faraway dream to them, but they believed in it and made it come true.

When I was little, my dream of becoming a world-class skater was far away, too. But I learned from my parents that if you work hard enough, your dream just might come true.

3

First Steps

I was born in southern California and have lived there my whole life. I love to feel warm and I hate the cold. So how did I fall in love with ice skating, anyway? I wish I knew!

I don't remember much of my life before skating. I remember playing with my stuffed animals when I was still home and Karen and Ron were at school. I know I loved candy, like most kids. But that's about it. It seems like I've been on the ice all my life.

When we were little, Karen and I went to gymnastics classes for a while. I guess that might have become my sport if Ron hadn't started playing ice hockey. Pretty soon Karen followed him to the rink. I wanted to skate too, but my parents wouldn't let me because they said I was too young.

I talked my parents' heads off about skating. I cried that it wasn't fair that I was being left out of the fun just because I was only five years old. Finally they couldn't take it anymore, I guess, and gave in.

Karen and I have always been best friends. And when we both became serious skaters, we spent morning, noon, and night together. But Ron has always been very independent. He did a little figure skating, but mostly he played hockey. And after that he got into all kinds of different sports — football, basketball, tennis. He's also the family comedian. When we were little, he'd come into our bedroom every night before Karen and I went to sleep and tell us the funniest jokes.

My parents used to make Ron walk us home from school every day. Ron was always in a big hurry to watch some show on TV, so he'd say to us, "There's a surprise for you at home! If you run, you can get it now!" Karen and I would run the whole way home to find out what it was. But the surprise would be something silly, like a flower that he said you could eat. It was just a trick he used to keep us from dawdling, and we always fell for it.

When we got home one of us would have to

squeeze through the little dog door and let the others in. (I don't remember why we didn't have house keys.) Since I was the smallest, I usually got that job. Then the three of us would race each other to our favorite place on the sofa. Everybody wanted the corner spot, with the soft pillow and the blanket. Whoever got there first was the winner — usually it was either me or Ron. We're both very competitive.

But most of the time I wasn't watching TV — I was skating. The rink we went to was in a shopping mall in Rolling Hills Estates, not far from our house in Rancho Palos Verdes. All of us had wobbly ankles at first, especially Karen, who's always had long flamingo legs. We wore rented brown skates that were ugly and stiff and hurt our feet, but we didn't care because we were having so much fun skating.

We took group lessons once a week. The first thing they taught us was how to fall, which I thought was funny. But now I know we needed to be able to fall without hurting ourselves. Then they taught us how to stand, how to hold on to the railing, and how to walk on the ice.

First things first, right? You've got to learn

the basics before you can go on to the more difficult and fun moves. If you're impatient like me, though, it's hard to wait.

Karen and I were both fast learners, and we were soon ready for more. After a couple of months of group lessons, I felt completely comfortable on my skates. I've always loved the feeling of moving on the ice — the faster the better. I remember during that first year being the smallest one on the ice and racing around offering Nerds candy to everyone.

After about six months, someone at the rink pulled me aside and said I should have private lessons. They pulled Karen aside, too. Maybe they pulled everyone aside; I don't know. But by then I *really* wanted private lessons, and soon I had a regular schedule at the rink.

Once I learned how to skate forward on the ice (the two parts to basic skating are *stroking* — pushing off of one foot — and *gliding*), I was ready to do waltz jumps and spirals and three-turns. All skaters have to learn how to do those basic fundamentals before they can even think about trying the more advanced skills like Axels, camels, and Salchows.

I was little and jumping came easily to me. I was so light that turning in the air one time took no effort at all. When I got bigger, I got stronger, which helped me jump higher in the air. But when I was small I didn't need to jump very high to do a revolution before landing again. It's still dangerous, though, and you should never try any of these tricks without a teacher.

It was in those early days at Rolling Hills Estates that I got my first taste of what it's like to fly. Even more than the jumping or spinning, I've always loved the pure feeling of simply stroking and gliding across the ice. I'd dig down into myself and take off across the ice as if it were a runway. I'd feel the wind in my face. Those are the times when I feel most like I'm flying — when my feet are still on the ground.

Ever since my first lesson, I've been impatient to learn more. I'm always saying, "Okay, I've got it. What's next?" I still feel that way. There are always new things to learn and ways to improve myself. That never stops, no matter how advanced I get. If it did, there would be no challenge.

When I was very little, I was happy playing with my stuffed animals and eating candy. And then things changed. I still liked toys and candy, but all I *really* wanted to do was skate.

4

My Olympic Dreams

Before long, skating took over most of my thoughts. I'd go to school wearing skating skirts, and I thought I was very cool to be doing something that none of my classmates did. Sitting at my desk, I would daydream about my next lesson at the rink.

Then, in 1988, when I was seven and a half, something really big happened — I watched the Winter Olympics on television. It was the year that Brian Boitano won the men's gold medal. I'd never seen anyone skate like *that* in Rolling Hills Estates. He was so elegant and so powerful and so disciplined.

I was really happy when he won the gold. I tried to imagine what he was feeling. Right then I decided that I wanted to know that feeling for *myself*. I vowed that *I* would go to the Olympics.

I started counting the years. At the 1994 Olympics I'd be thirteen (a teenager!). In 1998 I'd be seventeen (almost an adult!). In 2002, twenty-one years old (mature, sophisticated). In 2006 I'd be twenty-five. I told myself that I would be at all those Olympics. I didn't know that you had to qualify to get in. I thought you could just show up.

People find it hard to believe that I had that kind of determination at such a young age, but that's the way it happened. It wasn't just a one-night wish. I could *see* it happening. If I'd ever told myself it was an impossible dream, I never would have gotten this far.

I've always had a vivid imagination. I think it's one of my biggest strengths, because nothing seems impossible to me. But on the other hand, it can get a little out of control.

For instance, I'm afraid of the dark because I imagine things lurking in it. One night, looking out the window, I could swear I saw two men sitting in the trees. They looked like vampires — I'm not kidding! I shook my head, but my imagination had just taken over. I couldn't convince myself that it was just in my mind.

My imagination also tends to run a little wild when I'm swimming. I *love* to swim, but I'm scared of the water, especially oceans. Once when I was really little I nearly drowned in a swimming pool, so maybe that's why I'm afraid now.

But there's something else: I'm always sure there's a shark nearby, ready to get me. You'll think this is funny, but I'm even afraid of sharks in swimming pools! Once, my brother pinched me under water, and I actually thought for a minute that a shark had bitten me. Don't ever do that to me!

Actually, my imagination is working all the time, everywhere — even in my own bedroom. I have a lot of stuffed animals there, and all of them have distinct personalities. Sometimes it seems like they're really alive. Some, like my bears, Yellow Fuzzy-Wuzzy and Beary, can be trusted completely; others I'm not so sure about. I'm capable of imagining all kinds of crazy things about them.

My imagination works when I'm sleeping, too. Everybody's does. You probably won't be surprised to hear that I have a lot of really vivid dreams. This is another thing Karen and I share. More than once we've dreamed the same thing, even when we're thousands of miles apart. My mom always gets to hear our dreams in the morning.

One dream that keeps coming back to me is a dream about flying. Sometimes I fly like a bird, adjusting my arms like wings. I teach my friends how to fly, too.

And I still have my Olympic dream. That's as clear and bright as ever. I've never stopped imagining myself skating my very best in front of the world. It might be the closest I'll ever come to flying in real life.

5

Work Hard, Be Yourself, Have Fun

When I was seven, I didn't know what kind of commitment my love for skating would demand — not just from me, but from my whole family. But my parents could see it. When they saw that Karen and I were serious, they told us that so long as we really loved skating and were willing to work hard at it, they would do whatever it took to support our training. Over the years, they've had to learn as much about the sport as we have.

They've always told me, "Work hard, be yourself, and have fun." That's become my motto. It sounds simple, but it's a lot harder to *do* it than to *say* it. My parents make sure I work hard, but they also try to make sure I never forget to have fun. (My friends would

22

probably say, "As if Michelle would *ever* forget to have fun!")

After a few years at the rink in Rolling Hills Estates, Karen and I had learned everything they could teach us there — nothing more advanced than a single Axel. I felt impatient. I wanted to learn more and skate more. I was in a hurry to make my vision of being in the Olympics come true!

When I was about eight, my dad found a new teacher for Karen and me, a man named Derek James. He taught at a rink in Torrance, which is just north of Rancho Palos Verdes.

We skated four days a week at first with Derek, then five — in the mornings, after school, and on Wednesday nights. We had to wake up at four-thirty in the morning to be on the ice at five-thirty. We tried to give ourselves a few extra minutes so we could stop on the way to the rink and Dad could get doughnuts for Derek and the other skaters. Even though we were sleepy, we had fun those mornings.

Karen and I came up with the clever plan of sleeping in our skating clothes so that we could just roll out of bed, jump into the car, and pop onto the rink. The only problem was, sleeping in skating tights is *really* uncomfortable.

After a little while with Derek, we started competing at local rinks and skating clubs. Karen and I both did well. Sometimes she would win. Sometimes I would win. But, more often than not, a Kwan would win. Whether we won or lost, we always tried to do it with grace.

Some times it was easier to be graceful than others. Once when I skated out on the ice to start my program before a competition, I fell flat on my face! But I got right back up then, too.

At the same time, we were taking the tests to move up to higher levels within the ISIA (the Ice Skating Institute of America) and then the USFSA (the United States Figure Skating Association, the national governing body for figure skating in the United States).

My parents couldn't always afford our lessons with Derek, so we'd have to practice on our own sometimes. But the better our skating got, the more lessons we needed. Pretty soon, we qualified for regional and sectional competitions. Karen and I were so excited!

We were just kids, of course, so Mom or Dad had to take us to every competition. Since Dad was working hard for the phone company and Mom was working, too — in a factory for a while and then at the family restaurant — that meant that their schedules were even crazier than ours. Ron was very understanding when our parents were so busy with Karen and me.

As the competitions got bigger, the costumes got fancier and the traveling took longer. We were constantly asking ourselves, Are we really happy? Is this what we really want to do? The more we skated, the more the answers to those questions were YES and YES.

Of course, this meant that we couldn't do some of the things other kids were doing. We didn't have the extra time or the money. We used to save our change in an empty water-cooler bottle — the Kwan family piggy bank — and Mom would use that money for groceries and other necessary stuff.

One Christmas, my dad said we wouldn't be able to get a Christmas tree. He said it would only live a short time anyway, and we could do without it. I couldn't believe it! So I took matters into my own hands. I entered a contest at school: Whoever could make the longest string of popcorn in one minute got a fully decorated miniature tree. And I won! I got the cutest little tree.

But as I said, there wasn't much time to have fun outside of skating. We *all* had to be disciplined if Karen and I were going to skate seriously. Wherever we spun and jumped, our family was always right there behind us, even when things got tough. After we'd been training with Derek for a while, we ran out of money for skating lessons. For nine months we had to go without a coach, practicing instead with our parents or on our own.

Mom and Dad couldn't work any harder than they already were. Something had to change if we were going to be able to keep skating at this pace. So they sold our house in Rancho Palos Verdes, and we moved to a house our grandparents owned in Torrance. It would be a long time before we could afford a place of our own again.

Karen and I had to make some sacrifices, too. We wore hand-me-down clothes that three of our cousins had worn before we got them; we wore used skates and homemade costumes; we shared each other's skating tights. . . . But these were nothing like the sacrifices my grandfather and my father had to make when they were children.

Karen and I worked hard, not only at skating, but at school, too. We wanted to get good grades and to learn as much as we could. Our parents taught us that an education was a great opportunity that would come to us only once in life. We didn't want to miss it. It was fun to see our friends every day in class, but we always took our courses and our school-work very seriously.

In my house if we do something, we try not to do it halfway. We try not to let any opportunities pass us by.

My father didn't get to go to school until he was eight years old. When he was little he got up at four A.M. to wait by himself for a few pieces of meat for his family. Karen and I had to get up at four-thirty, but it was to do something we loved. To go ice skating! To try to make our dreams come true! What's more, we had each other.

Sometimes I'll be out there on the ice, shivering. My muscles ache and my face feels so cold it's about to fall off. But if I start to feel sorry for myself, I stop and remind myself that I'm there only because I *want* to be. Nobody else is making me do it. "Work hard, be yourself, and have fun." That's all my parents have ever asked of me.

6

Sisters/Buddies

Karen and I did *everything* together. We were together on the ice, off the ice, in the morning, in the evening. We were constantly talking — in bed, at the rink . . . in the bathroom.

Sometimes we competed at different levels, sometimes at the same level. Karen would take a skating test and rise to a level higher than me, but pretty soon I'd catch up with her and we'd be even again for a while.

I don't think we've ever really felt competitive toward each other. For one thing, I've always looked up to Karen and admired her. And each of us is a totally unique person. If you look at us today, you can see how different we are.

To start with, we don't look alike. Karen is 5'8" and I'm the shorty — 5'2". The skaters at our rink used to call me "Little Kwan" and Karen "Big Kwan."

When we were little kids we often wore matching outfits. But that didn't last long. Karen has always had a really good sense of style and fashion. She likes trendy clothes. With her tall, slender body and long legs she looks great in everything. Long skirts, miniskirts, all kinds of funky combinations.

She also makes some of her own clothes. She's been known to take something she bought and cut off a sleeve or change the neckline. She's not afraid to try new or wacky things.

I'm short and I can't wear all the clothes Karen does. I gave up trying to dress like her when I was about thirteen. I love clothes as much as she does, but now I have my own style.

My style is more classic and simple than Karen's. Sometimes I like preppy-looking things. Most of all I like clothes that are beautifully made and fit me perfectly. I'm too small for the baggy look — I get lost in those enormous blue jeans. The one area where I go crazy is with lipstick and nail polish. I love trying all kinds of wild colors.

Even though we've trained together all our

lives, Karen and I don't skate alike. Karen skates like a ballerina. When we were younger, I used to watch her with those long, elegant legs and graceful arms, and I wished I could get that kind of feeling into my skating.

In the past couple of years I've worked really hard on my programs. Now I have a reputation as an "artistic" skater, and maybe the differences between us aren't as great as when we were little. Basically I have a more aggressive, more athletic style than Karen.

I'm organized, and I need schedules and discipline. Karen has a more dreamy personality. She has lots of different talents, not just skating. She's really funny and smart, and she has a great eye for design — in architecture, clothes, and pictures.

We have different attitudes about skating, too. I've always been very competitive. The first time I skated in the U.S. Senior Nationals, I was twelve years old, and I came in sixth. I was unbelievably happy that night. But afterward all I could think about was how to do better next year. In 1996 Karen finished fifth in the Nationals. Afterward she told me that she felt lucky to have done so well. She was really happy with that fifth.

I try hard to have that kind of perspective.

But I can't help thinking, Just a little more effort and I'll do even better. I'm an *extremely* competitive person — above all, with myself.

When we were kids, Karen was very feminine. I was more of a tomboy. I liked to play really fierce games like handball and dodgeball. In dodgeball, which I *loved*, I was always the last one standing.

Karen and I are different all right, but we know each other through and through. I swear I can always tell what she's thinking. She's away at college now, and she seems to know when I'm going to call her. If she goes out, she'll leave a message for me on her answering machine: "If this is you, Michelle . . ."

We also know everything about each other's skating. When we were little we knew each other's programs inside out. (We still do.) If Karen skated right before me in a competition, I couldn't watch her because I had to concentrate on my own program. But I could hear her music and the audience. I knew where all the hardest jumps were, so if I heard clapping at that place in the music, I knew she was doing well.

If I skated before her, I could watch her program. That's almost harder than doing the skating myself. There's nothing I can do to

31

help her, and I hate that. My parents have to go through this with both of us all the time! It's torture. My heart just freezes. I grit my teeth. But if she does well, I'm as happy for her as I would be for myself.

Karen has always been my closest buddy and my best supporter. She's been a big part of my success. She's helped me with all three parts of "Work hard, be yourself, and have fun." Without Karen around all the time, it would have taken me a lot longer to know who "myself" really was.

We knew we could always count on each other, and together we were an unbeatable team. But as we got older, the stakes got higher and the competitions got tougher. Then we needed to be able to stand on our own, too, and know exactly who we were.

7

A Giant Leap

When you're a young skater, one of the most exciting things is moving up to a new level in the USFSA. Each level is a stepping stone to becoming a Senior Lady skater. And you have to be a Senior skater to compete with the best skaters in the world.

Every level has its own basic skill requirements. There's Pre-Preliminary, Preliminary, Pre-Juvenile, Juvenile, Intermediate, Novice, and Junior. Every time you move up, you get a little pin, and you become eligible to compete with other skaters at that level.

By 1992 Karen and I were both Junior skaters. From there, becoming a Senior seemed like a little hop away. I could almost see it, just over a little hill.

I'd already learned to do most of the triple jumps, even the Lutz and the flip, which are the two most difficult ones that women skaters attempt. Later I'd have some trouble with the Lutz, but would you believe that I got it the first time I ever tried it?

Once Karen and I got up to the Junior level, we needed more than five days on the ice. We couldn't go to the Torrance rink more than we already were because it was busy with hockey on the weekends. So my parents came up with another idea.

Some friends of ours lived in the San Bernardino Mountains in a town called Lake Arrowhead, 100 miles outside of Los Angeles. A world-famous ice-skating facility called Ice Castle was there, and they had open skating sessions every day of the week. My parents started driving us up there on the weekends to skate.

Ice Castle has two different rinks. We went to the public rink, where anyone can skate. It's a really pretty place. When you're skating you see giant pine trees all around on three sides, because the walls don't reach up to the roof!

A little ways down the main road, then up a narrow winding lane, is Ice Castle's private world-class training facility. Only elite skaters and kids who are working with Ice Castle coaches can use it. The great world champion, Lu Chen, along with Surya Bonaly, the five-time European champion, and lots of other top-level skaters have all trained there.

Not that I was in the same league with Lu and Surya yet; but I was dying to skate with them. I was so excited every time I arrived in Lake Arrowhead because I felt close to my skating dreams.

And then things began to happen that would bring me a lot closer to them.

I had an amazing season in 1992. First I won the gold medal at the Southwest Pacific Regionals. That qualified me for the Pacific Coast Sectionals, where I got the bronze. And *that* got me into my first national competition: the Junior Nationals.

Karen had already skated in a national competition — at the Novice level, the year before. Now, it was *my* turn to go to Nationals.

I was skating really well, but it all happened so fast that we could hardly believe it. I wasn't ready for a national competition! We hadn't been able to afford a coach for nine months. In those days we didn't have any money at all. Selling the house paid off the bills, but after that there wasn't much left.

Luckily we had a few "godparents" looking out for us, people who helped us with money and all kinds of support when things got tough. When I was about ten and Karen was twelve, a man named Steve Hazen saw us skating at a competition. He told us how much he liked our skating, and he said he'd like to help us if he could. Pretty soon he was one of our best friends. He and his wife, Ming Li, became just like family members to us.

George Steinbrenner, the owner of the New York Yankees and a former vice president of the USOC (United States Olympic Committee), has helped out lots of athletes. He gave me a lot of support. So did our friend Helen McLaughlin, who is another skating lover and very active in the skating world. Then, when I desperately needed a coach to help me prepare for the Junior Nationals, a kind of miracle happened.

Virginia Fratianne, mother of the great skater Linda Fratianne, had seen me skate at Ice Castle and in some of the competitions. She knew me and Karen, and had always taken an interest in us. When she heard about my spot in the Nationals, she talked to her friends up at Ice Castle about us.

Linda's coach was a man named Frank Carroll. He was considered one of the greatest coaches there was. He worked at Ice Castle with some of the best skaters in the world. Virginia told him about me and Karen and arranged for each of us to have a lesson with him. It would be a kind of audition to see if Frank wanted to work with us.

My lesson was on a Friday. I was so nervous. I really wanted to impress Frank. I wasn't sure if I belonged with the top skaters Frank coached, but something inside me told me' that I might. I guess Frank agreed. I skated well for him, and he took me on as his pupil. Karen did well, too. We were both going to become students of Frank Carroll. We were so excited!

Later Frank would tell me that he knew just by watching me that first time that I had the potential to be a world champion. He said he hadn't had a feeling like that since the first time he saw Linda Fratianne skate. I had the "spark," he said.

I felt like I was on my way to the big time. I knew we had our work cut out for us, because Junior Nationals were only three weeks away. But I thought I'd just keep rolling, like I had been all season.

Well, it turns out I had a lot to learn. I was about to get a painful lesson about skating at the highest levels. It might have been my first lesson, but it definitely would not be my last.

8

Ice Castle Heaven

A whole new world was about to open up to me, Karen, and our entire family. With Virginia's and Frank's help, Karen and I were accepted as students at the private rink at Ice Castle.

As if that weren't exciting enough, we got scholarships that covered a lot of our expenses. We would live at Ice Castle all year long. We'd eat there, go to school there, and skate there *seven days a week*. It was a dream come true for Karen and me.

Ice Castle is an amazing place. It used to be a camp, so it has lots of cabins (twenty-four to be exact) and a big dormitory that can sleep more than seventy kids. There's a dance pavilion, a swimming pool, a Jacuzzi, a gym, and, of course, the indoor ice rink — one of the best in the world.

It's all set among giant cedar and pine trees, and tucked into the mountains 5,100 feet above sea level. In the winter the branches sag from the weight of the snow. In the spring and summer, when the flowers are in bloom and the fish are jumping, it seems like the most beautiful place on earth. It's very quiet, so it's perfect for serious work . . . and serious dreaming.

Ice Castle was founded and run by Walter Probst and his wife, Carol Caverly Probst, who used to skate in the Ice Follies. They were so nice to me from the very beginning and have helped me so much since then that I can't imagine where I'd be without them. Add them to the list of my godparents.

The Ice Castle rink is encircled by a rubberized floor, but there are no rink-boards (the waist-high walls that go around most rinks). You just step right off the floor and onto the ice. One wall has a floor-to-ceiling mirror. Parents and visitors sit at the other end. If they want to watch practice they have to stay there in their own special area. That's so the coaches can work with their students without having to worry about parents butting in!

There's also a harness that hangs from the ceiling and can slide across the surface of the ice. We strap ourselves into it when we're learning new jumps that are especially difficult — like the triple Axel — so that we don't get hurt. Some jumps are extremely dangerous and difficult. If you skate, you should never try them without the supervision of a teacher.

Every day there are lots of practice sessions, when groups of skaters work with their coaches or practice on their own. Usually the ice isn't too crowded. But in the summer, when there are a lot more skaters, you really have to watch where you're going so you don't crash into anyone.

Three times a day the elite skaters get their forty-five-minute sessions. You see them whizzing around together, spinning, jumping, skating backward. Amazingly, they seldom run into each other.

This was the new world we'd landed in. All of a sudden, everyone we knew was a skater, a skater's mom, or a skating coach. All we talked about was skating. We ate all our meals in the "lodge" on the campus. For the first year, we went to the public school in Lake Arrowhead with the other skaters. (After that, I had private tutors.) We were living the total skating life.

Like I said, Frank only had three weeks to get me ready for Junior Nationals. I think maybe he found out he had more work than he had counted on. I was a mess! It was embarrassing. It wasn't until I got to Ice Castle and saw how serious skaters worked that I realized what a rookie I was.

I really had no idea of how to train with someone like Frank. I had lots of bad habits. I thought I knew something about discipline, but I didn't really. In those three weeks, I found out just how much I could learn from Frank.

The first thing I learned was that when you work on your program, you have to keep going even if you fall — just like you have to do when you're competing. You can't give up every time you make a mistake. You have to get right back up and learn how to work *through* mistakes. You can't sit there and whine about the fact that you fell.

Frank says falling in practice is a great opportunity. You may never have another chance to practice how to recover at that exact moment in the program ever again.

I was doing a lot of triple jumps already, but not consistently. Most of them were hit or miss, and that won't do. I have to be able to do a jump eighty percent of the time in practice, or else Frank won't put it in my program.

Even though I was excited, I did start to feel pretty nervous as Nationals got nearer. One night in our cabin, my dad heard me talking in my sleep. I was dreaming about skating and trying to calm myself down, I guess, by saying, "It's nothing. It's nothing. It's nothing. . . ."

Dad felt worried and sad to hear me talking like that. The next morning he gave me a hug and told me he was proud of how hard I was working. He told me how happy it made him to see Karen and me skating so well, but he said I shouldn't work so hard that I couldn't enjoy it. "There's a fine line between discipline and pressure," he said, and I should be careful not to cross it.

Frank did the best he could with me in the short time that we had to prepare together. And then we went off to Florida for the competition. I felt ready. To tell you the truth, by that time I may even have been a bit overconfident. I had done so well at the regionals and

43

sectionals, I thought I'd just keep winning. I wasn't prepared for the pressure or the fierceness of the competition. It was like nothing I'd seen before.

There's no minimum or maximum age to be a Junior skater. Once you pass the test, you can compete at that level whatever your age. You can be a Junior and be over twenty! I was only eleven, so I was one of the very youngest.

Some of the girls at the competition looked like grown women. They wore makeup and fancy costumes. In those days, and for a few years after, I didn't wear any makeup. I just pulled my hair back in a ponytail and went out onto the ice as I was: a kid.

Finally the big moment came. I was about to skate in my first Nationals. But hold on! Just before my short program, Frank looked at my skates and turned pale. They were covered with smudges and streaks. I hadn't polished them in months.

I thought it would bring me good luck if I left them just the way they were after the sectionals. I didn't realize it mattered to anyone. I had all kinds of rituals and superstitions back then. Wearing dirty skates was just one of them.

Well, Frank screamed. He said I couldn't go on the ice like that. It was an insult to the judges. I didn't have any polish in my skate bag, so Frank ran around backstage calling out, "Does anyone have boot polish? I need boot polish!"

He found some and went to work polishing my boots on his knees. It was so embarrassing. The other coaches were laughing. He was working away, blowing on the boots to dry them, when my name was called. My boots were still wet when I took the ice.

I had some problems in the short program that were more serious than the condition of my skates — in particular, my triple toe-loop. The truth is, both of my programs were disasters. It was nothing like at the sectionals, where everything had gone so smoothly. Here, everything went wrong. It was a shock to me. I'd expected to skate perfectly, but I skated worse than I ever had, and I finished ninth. Afterward I cried like a baby.

I think Frank knew that I'd been feeling too confident, and he kind of let me figure that out for myself. Looking back, I think he was trying to teach me a lesson I really needed to learn. The lesson was about discipline and how you

45

can never, *never* take anything for granted in
this sport.

I did learn a lot from those Nationals, but the
whole thing also made me mad. I knew I could
skate better than that, and I wanted another
chance. Soon!

9

The Secret Test

Okay, so I learned a lot from my experience in Junior Nationals. But even after bombing there, I still believed in myself. *I* knew I was a much better skater than that. Not just a better Junior skater — I thought I was ready to become a Senior skater, at the age of twelve.

As usual, I was impatiently thinking ahead. It was nice that Karen and I were skating at the same level, but if I didn't take the test now so that I could qualify my way into the 1993 Senior Nationals, I'd never make it to the 1994 Olympics. Karen was working hard as a Junior and didn't feel ready to move up to the highest level yet. But I really did feel ready — even if I had to move up without her.

I had this burning desire to compete in the big time. To be out there with Lu Chen

and Surya Bonaly and Nancy Kerrigan. To
compete with Tonya Harding, the only American woman who could do a triple Axel. I
knew myself, and I knew my skating. I didn't
see why I couldn't do it.

Others did. Frank, for one. He said the thing
to do was to wait. If we worked hard all year,
I'd have a good chance of winning the Junior
Nationals in 1993. Frank said the judges like
to get to know a skater before they give them
high scores at Seniors competitions. They like
to know you've paid your dues.

Frank went off to a coaches' conference in
Canada for a week. And I did something that I
don't usually do: I ignored the wisdom of
someone who was older and wiser than me
and I took the Senior test. This is a good ex-
ample of what I mean when I say I'm impatient. I do have a mind of my own, and at that
moment I felt like I knew me and my abilities
better than anyone else.

My dad asked me if Frank said it was all right
for me to take the test. I didn't exactly lie, but
I think I kind of mumbled my answer and
maybe gave Dad the impression that Frank
said it was okay.

Anyway, we went to Los Angeles to take the
test. All I had to do was skate my program for

a panel of judges. If I could do all the skills the USFSA required for Senior skaters in competitions, they move me on up. Easy as pie. I'd get my little pin, and go home as a *Lady* skater. After that, I couldn't skate at the lower levels anymore.

I passed, no problem, like I expected. But then came the hard part. I had to tell Frank.

Frank is one of the greatest coaches in the world. I already had a huge amount of respect for him. At the same time, I couldn't resist a challenge. When he came home, I explained to him that the challenge of becoming a top-level skater and maybe getting into the 1994 Olympics was irresistible to me. I hoped he'd understand.

All the same, he flipped his lid. He was furious. For a few days he wouldn't talk to me. He didn't think I was ready for the big leagues. He thought I'd skate onto the ice in my first Senior competition, and the judges would say, "Who is this *kid*?"

Things were bad between us for a while. I apologized and apologized, and hoped he would calm down.

When he finally did, he sat me down and said, "Young lady, you have no idea what it means to be a Senior skater. You know next to nothing about the artistic side of skating. You need to understand how to *hear* the music. You are going to have to *transform* your skating."

I took it all in. Frank was right, of course. I was a good jumper, but my skating wasn't elegant or beautiful. And I hadn't thought that much about really *listening* to the music. I just got out there and jumped around.

Frank said I would have to be a perfectionist in every aspect of my presentation. My costumes, my hair, my face. My spirals, my edges, my footwork. He asked if I had any idea of the work I had ahead of me. I told him that *now* I did, and that I would do whatever I had to do . . . whatever he told me to do.

My parents listened to what Frank said, too. My mom was worried that I wasn't ready for this next big step. My dad reminded me of the thin line between discipline and pressure. Although they both wanted me to have discipline, they were afraid I was too young for the kind of pressure I'd face.

But my parents said that if I wanted it with all my heart, and if I was ready for the hard work ahead, they'd back me up like they always had. And they'd keep an eye on me to make sure I was still having fun and being my-self.

I did want it, and I did feel ready. The judges gave me a pin that said I was a Senior skater. But I wouldn't really be one until I could make myself one. So that's what I set out to do. Like I said, I *love* a challenge.

10

What It Takes

Now that I'd made the leap to the Senior level, it wasn't enough anymore to be a talented kid. All of a sudden I would be compared to the best skaters in the world. I had to study them and think about the ones who came before me, like Peggy Fleming and Dorothy Hamill, Janet Lynn and Linda Fratianne.

I would need to take parts from all of them. Peggy Fleming's grace and artistry. Brian Boitano's heart. Dorothy Hamill's elegance.

Every skater has qualities that make him or her special. When I was little, my jumping made me stand out. I had good "spring," which means I could get up high in the air without seeming to make much effort. At a very young age I was able to do the triple jumps that most skaters don't get till they're older.

But my programs were simple. I was young and I looked it. I had a lot of work ahead of me to bring my programs up to the level of the elite skaters. In a great program, every movement should flow naturally into the next one. The music and skating should seem like they were meant for each other. The music should seem to *fill* the skater, just like it fills the arena.

Each skater has two programs for competitions. There's the "technical" or "short program," which is two minutes and thirty seconds long. And there's the "freeskate" or "long program," which is four minutes long for women (four and a half for men). The long program is by far the more important of the two. That's where "artistry" counts most.

The judges look for many required elements in a program. If the skater leaves any out, they deduct points from the score. You have to make sure the judges see those elements, but you can't interrupt the flow of the program to point at yourself and say, "*Look at this!*"

Spirals and spread eagles, which are harder to do well than you might think, show off edges, balance, flexibility, and speed. But they have to seem effortless and smooth.

Spins can be more tiring than jumps. You have to use all your muscles to hold your body tight in order to get the most revolution and speed that you can while staying centered on one spot. You have to be able to step out of a spin and into the next part of your program as if it's the easiest thing in the world.

As with spins, the most difficult and athletic jumps take great strength. You have to have speed going into your jump and speed coming out of it. You need power in your legs to push yourself high into the air.

But a skater's mind has to be strong, too, and focused. It shouldn't look to the judges like this triple Lutz is any more difficult than anything else you've done. With combination jumps, the second one has to follow the first one smoothly.

Look at three-time world champion Elvis Stojko. He does quadruple/triple combinations. That's *seven revolutions*, total! It's amazingly difficult, but he makes it look simple.

When I started as a Senior, my programs were bumpy. The jumps and the steps and the spins weren't connected. I didn't let the music help me flow from one move to another. I didn't understand about *interpreting* the music. I rarely even smiled when I skated back then. To get to the level of great artists like Peggy,

Dorothy, and Brian, you have to be *both* an athlete and an artist.

Most elite skaters have three forty-five-minute long practice sessions on the ice every day, usually with their coaches. They spend at least another hour in a gym making their muscles stronger and more flexible. On top of that, they work "on the floor" with their coaches, practicing jumps without the momentum and speed the ice gives them. They spend hours and hours with their choreographers developing new programs.

At the end of a day like this your body aches everywhere. Your back hurts from doing layback spins. Your bottom hurts from falling. Your shoulders, your legs — you just hurt all over. But there's still more to do.

Every month there's at least one major competition, plus exhibitions. The most important competitions come in the late winter and early spring. Nationals are in January or February and Worlds are in March. And in an Olympic year, the Olympics take place between Nationals and Worlds. So you can see, there's hardly any time between the competitions to take a breath!

There are costumes to be fitted and fixed —

costumes are my mother's speciality (she works together with Maré Talbot on mine). But aside from practice clothes and gloves, the only piece of equipment a skater needs is her skates. (A warning about gloves: Skaters use them to wipe their noses, which run like crazy on an ice rink. Never borrow a skater's gloves!)

Most skaters use just one pair of skates all year long. They usually get a new pair at the beginning of the season, and it takes weeks and weeks to break them in. Sometimes it takes all season to get them just right. When I first start using new skates, it's agony. Most skaters have really ugly feet. You should see how swollen and gnarled my toes are when I take off my skates. On second thought, you don't want to!

I'd always worn used skates and didn't get an actual brand-new pair of skates until 1995 (they're expensive!). A skater has to pick out the right boot and then put the blade on with screws.

My father is good with skates. For years he cut the heels of my boots lower for me so that my weight wouldn't go too far forward. And he always has to fiddle with the blade, making sure it's placed properly.

Sometimes everything feels different in new skates. Your weight is distributed differently. Your balance feels strange. A jump that was no problem at all last year is suddenly impossible — until you figure out how to adjust yourself to new skates.

Adjustment is something young skaters have to deal with just about every day. Our bodies are always changing. Not only do we get taller all the time, but as we get older we find a pound or two in places we never even noticed before. Luckily the changes don't usually happen overnight. When we're on the ice every day, we can adjust to them gradually.

I *love* moving across the ice. So I didn't mind when I started to get a little bigger and stronger because I could put some real weight into my edges and increase my speed. I was able to really *cover* the surface of the ice. That's when I feel most like I'm flying.

Another change that happened when I became a Senior skater was that I had the chance to be noticed by the millions of people who watch skating on TV.

If you're an amateur and eligible to compete in all the major competitions, like the Olympics, that doesn't mean you can't do *any* professional work. There are professional competitions and exhibitions throughout the year that the USFSA allows eligible skaters to do, and some of them pay very well.

Money wasn't in the picture for *me* yet, though. If anything, the cost of training went up then — by a lot. The scholarships that Karen and I received paid for our living expenses and ice-time at Ice Castle. The USFSA gave us some support, too. But we had to pay Frank and buy skates. We also each had to have three costumes a year. Plus it was expensive to travel to the competitions — which, now that I was a Senior, were all over the world!

The life of a top-level skater is intense. A lot of skaters get so overwhelmed by it that they can't even think about their schoolwork. Many drop out of school. But I'd never want to do that, and my parents would never let me.

While all of this new activity was going on, I also had to study. I went to a regular school until the eighth grade when I became a Senior skater and my schedule got crazy. Since then I've had a tutor, who comes to my house. But that doesn't mean I have it easy. I still have to take tests and do homework (lots of it!), just like everybody else.

One of the most difficult and important

challenges of being a full-time skater at such a young age is remembering that skating isn't everything. You have to work hard to remember that you're just at the very *beginning* of your life. People may call you a "Lady" or a "woman skater" or a "Senior," but you can't forget that you're really still a kid. And you can never forget how important school is.

That's why I've always tried to carry two images of myself in my mind. There's the picture of the skater I dream of being. But skating is only a sport, after all, and you should only do it if you really love it. The bigger picture I keep in mind is of the *person* I want to be and the life I want to live. That's the real challenge.

11

The Big Time

I was twelve years old during my first season as a Senior skater. I tried hard to lead a normal life, but it wasn't easy. I was running all the time — working, skating, doing homework, and trying to spend time with my family. There weren't enough hours in the day. What a life for a twelve year old. But I loved it!

When we moved to the Ice Castle campus, we had to do a little shuffling around. My mother stayed in Torrance with Ron so that he could finish high school there and she could run the restaurant with my grandparents. My dad stayed with Karen and me in our cabin on the campus and commuted to work every day. He had to get up very early in order to make the 100-mile drive "down the hill."

Every night he drove back up, and boy was he tired when he got home.

I missed my mom a lot. It's a good thing I was so busy doing something I loved so much, or else I would have really been sad without her. But being apart so much did something good, too — it made the time we had together seem even more special and exciting.

On the weekends, we'd go down the hill to Torrance, or else my mom would come up and stay with us. Ron came to visit, too. Even though our family had this crazy schedule, Ron still acted like a normal big brother when he came to visit. He loved to tease me, pinch me, and generally pick on me. If you have a big brother, you know exactly what I mean!

We lived in a little cabin called the "Debi Thomas Teepee," named after the American 1988 Olympic bronze medalist. It was just one small room for the three of us, but to Karen and me it seemed cozy and fun.

Karen and I thought living in the cabin was a great adventure. We had lots of friends and were busy all the time. We even tried to have pets. For a while we had a squirrel, then some hamsters, then a dog, and then a bird. But we never had much luck with our pets, and none of them stayed around for very long. Bad things were always happening to them. For instance, the hamsters kept having babies until there were dozens of them. Then one day they got out of the cage and escaped — after we'd chased them all over the room.

There really wasn't time to take care of pets, anyway. Karen was busy competing at the Junior level. And since it was my first year as a Senior, I had to go through all the qualifying rounds of the competitions. I won both the Senior regionals and sectionals, so things were looking good. Most importantly I earned my spot in my first Senior Nationals.

The 1993 Nationals were held in Phoenix, Arizona. All the top skaters were there. When I showed up for practice I saw the reigning champion, Tonya Harding, as well as Nancy Kerrigan. I was slated to skate right after Tonya. Just being on the same ice with her while she practiced her triple Axel felt weird and exciting, like I was in a movie.

Although I'd been skating really well in practice, I missed a couple of jumps in my long program. Still, everyone was happy for me. They were surprised I had done as well as I had. "You're so cute, Michelle," I kept hearing.

— Nancy Kerrigan won, and I finished sixth. Even though I hadn't skated my best, sixth place was a decent finish. I felt sure that if I kept working, I could do a lot better next year. Maybe well enough to make it into the Olympics.

The rest of the season after Nationals was great. I made my first trip out of the country, to Italy, to compete in something called the Gardena Spring Trophy. I'd never skated with girls from other countries before. Meeting skaters from Russia and Germany and other places was exciting. It was a beautiful setting, too, kind of like Lake Arrowhead, with mountains and tall trees and lots of quiet. But it was also completely different, because it felt exotic and wonderful to be in another country. To be in Europe!

Then I skated at a competition called the Olympic Festival, which is one of my all-time favorite skating memories. It was held at the enormous Alamodome in San Antonio, Texas, and there were more than 25,000 people in the audience! I'd never skated for a crowd that big. It was awesome to be all alone on the ice, feeling very small down there, and then to hear roaring cheers coming from the stands all around me.

I definitely felt like I was flying at the Alamo-dome. It was like a dream. And even better because I won the gold medal there!

I hope moments like that aren't just exciting for me, but for my whole family, too. All of us were working so hard. My dad was so tired at the end of each day that I worried about him. My mom didn't get to see us at all during the week, and we missed each other a lot. Our lives were so complicated. We had fun whenever we were all together, but how were my parents feeling during the other times?

I loved the attention I got when I skated, and I was more than happy I'd become a Senior skater. It's what I'd wished for my whole life. But I wondered about my parents. Were they happy? They told me about the thin line between discipline and pressure — but were they careful about that, too?

As for me, the closer I came to the things I'd wished for, the thinner that line became. I was about to learn the meaning of the old saying, "Be careful what you wish for. You just might get it."

12

My Strangest Year

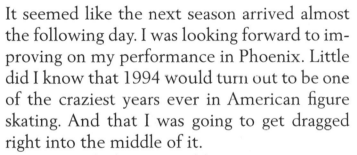

It seemed like the next season arrived almost the following day. I was looking forward to improving on my performance in Phoenix. Little did I know that 1994 would turn out to be one of the craziest years ever in American figure skating. And that I was going to get dragged right into the middle of it.

Karen took the test and became a Senior — hooray! — so we were skating at the same level again. She didn't qualify for Nationals, though, so once again (and for the last time), I was the only skater representing the Kwan family at the U.S. Championships. This year they were held in Detroit, Michigan.

Just before Nationals, Karen told me that she had a dream that I came in second and that Nancy Kerrigan withdrew from the competition. It seemed like a crazy dream. Nancy was the defending champion — everyone thought she was going to win — and she wasn't going to withdraw after all her hard work! Even if she did, Tonya Harding and Nicole Bobek and lots of skaters more experienced than me would be there, too.

The oldest skater in competition was Elaine Zayak, who was twenty-nine and had won a national championship the year after I was born! Nancy was twenty-four. Tonya was twenty-three. I was thirteen — once again, the baby. Everyone kept telling me how *cute* I was. I hate being called "cute"!

Right before the competition, Nancy and I were in the same group for practice time. I could see what great shape she was in. After practice, I left the ice just ahead of her. I stopped to put the guards on my blades, and someone called, "Nancy, Nancy! Can I have your autograph?"

I let Nancy go on ahead of me, and she disappeared behind a big curtain that separated the backstage area from the audience. Then I heard her scream. It sounded like she'd fallen. Someone pushed me aside and ran to help her. Parents and coaches rushed past the curtain to her. I had no idea what was going on. When I went in, I saw her on the ground, crying and holding her leg. I didn't find out about what had happened till later.

Now, of course, everyone knows that Nancy was struck in the knee by an acquaintance of Jeff Gillooly, Tonya Harding's husband — but then no one knew about any of that. All they knew was that Nancy had been injured in an attack, and she wouldn't be able to skate. The place turned into a circus. Reporters were everywhere.

I didn't skate my best in the long program. I knew, once again, that I could have done much better. When would I ever get my act together to prove it at Nationals? But because Nancy had withdrawn, I was able to finish second, right behind Tonya. So as one of the top two finishers, I was on the Olympic team . . . for one brief moment.

In a completely bizarre way, Karen's dream turned out to be closer to the truth than I'd ever thought possible. I was glad to be second, but not happy about the way I got there.

Standing on the podium with my silver medal was still an exciting moment. I couldn't help enjoying myself. Standing up there with Tonya. Seeing my parents in the crowd. All the people cheering for us. It was a thrill.

Later on, the USFSA decided that Nancy — not me — would get to go to the Olympics, even though she hadn't competed at Nationals. I wasn't surprised. I thought that was fair and Nancy deserved to go. She'd been working for it all year. It wasn't her fault that someone had attacked her. Since there were only two spots for the team at the Olympics, that meant it was going to be Nancy and Tonya.

But not so quick! Rumors about Tonya and her husband started going around. Everyone was fascinated by the story, which was all over the TV and in the newspapers. The USFSA and the USOC were watching, too. They wanted to find out whether or not there was proof that Tonya had been involved.

The Olympics were right around the corner. A decision wouldn't be made until everyone got to Norway. So they called me up and told me to pack my bag. I was going as an alternate!

The reporters heard that and suddenly wanted *me*. Little Michelle Kwan was hot news! They came to Lake Arrowhead and camped out outside Ice Castle. They followed me everywhere. They snuck into the rink, trying to chase me down.

It was too much. We had to hide from the reporters, and I could hardly think about skating. The TV show *Hard Copy* and the tabloid newspapers were calling and knocking on the door. My parents didn't know what to tell them. Even Frank didn't know how to deal with all those people. We needed more help. So my parents decided to call Shep Goldberg.

Shep is a sports manager. The great Olympic gymnastics champion Mary Lou Retton is his client. He had called us a couple of times and said that if we ever needed him, we should let him know. Well, now we needed him. Shep came straight to Lake Arrowhead and started getting things under control. And that's how I got a manager, who is now one of my best friends. Shep goes almost everywhere with me and takes very good care of me.

Just when I thought the media circus was over, I went to the airport to go to Norway. A swarm of reporters was standing outside my gate. Someone told me that David Hasselhoff, the TV star, was on my flight. I figured they were there for him. But no. They were there for *me*.

I didn't know what to say to all those reporters! "What about Nancy?" they asked. "What about Tonya?" Shep told me just to be myself and tell the truth. Since I had no idea what was going to happen in Norway, the truthful answer to most of their questions was "I don't know."

In the end, I didn't get to compete in the Olympics. I didn't even get to stay in the Olympic Village — my hotel was outside the village, which was kind of lonely. But I did get a chance to go to Norway and I *did* go to the Olympics, after all, like I vowed I would. I was in the stands watching and not on the ice skating rink, but technically speaking, my dream did come true. Besides, in a few weeks I'd have my chance to be the one on the ice with the whole world watching me.

13

My First Worlds

So far, 1994 had been a year in which a small part of my dream had come true — just not the way I'd planned. I'd been to the Olympics (kind of) and I'd become a little bit famous (by accident).

But there was one more surprise in store for me: at my very first world championships I would be the *entire* United States women's team.

After Nancy won the silver medal at the Olympics, barely losing the gold to Oksana Baiul, she decided she'd been through enough. She announced that she would not go to the Worlds in Chiba, Japan, that year. Tonya stayed home, too, because she'd resigned from amateur skating.

That meant that I had a big responsibility at Worlds. In order to secure two spots for our team in *next* year's Worlds, I had to finish in the top ten. It was all up to me.

At thirteen, I was the youngest ever to compete for the U.S. in the world championships. Everyone was keeping their fingers crossed, hoping I could handle the pressure.

I'd been working hard and had lots of people giving me advice. For a while I had some extra help from Irina Rodnina, who is a ten-time world-champion pairs skater and a legend in the skating world. She helped me improve my stroking power and the flow in my program. We desperately needed to pump me up — to make the judges believe that I was more than *cute*, that I was mature and good enough to rank in the top ten in the world.

I had trouble in my technical program with my triple Lutz. Going into the freeskate, I was in *eleventh* place. But I stayed calm. I told myself to forget about placing and about all those other expectations. The most important thing to remember was *my* expectation for myself, which was to skate my best. Period.

The whole world was watching me now. They didn't care what I had to say about

Three years old...
wearing my favorite pin
from my grandma

Two years old...
posing with Ron + Karen

Seven years old... My mom was so proud, she had to take a picture of me with my first trophy.

My first time winning three gold medals

Karen + me posing in matching outfits

Joking around and dressing up as Santa Claus
for the Christmas show

Standing in front of the Olympic Training Center
thinking of my Olympic dreams

Trying to prove myself at the 1994 nationals.

I was so happy to win the silver medal at nationals.
I was hoping to make the Olympic team.

I was going to the Olympics — suddenly
I was hot news!

Being cozy with my stuffed animals

Doing a spiral at the 1995 nationals in Providence, Rhode Island

Thumbs-up after a good performance at Nationals

In London at the 1995 Worlds, and of course, it's raining!

My buddy Harris and me on the bus

Me + Kristi Yamaguchi

Brian Boitano - one of my most favorite people in the world

Dad and me having fun

1996 Christmas—for the first time in a long while, Ron, Karen and I spent time together

The three Kwan females living it up in Paris

Practicing jumps with Frank

Finding my beginning pose with Lori Nichol, my choreographer

Scared and determined to stay on the boat

In Alaska I caught the biggest fish of my life ..... 25 lbs.

Right after my most difficult move in Salome, the triple lutz

Striking my beginning pose for Taj Majal

I was so happy and proud when I won Worlds.

Posing with my support group – my mom, Lori Nichol, Frank, Mrs. Probst, and my dad, after the 1996 Worlds

My friends threw a party for me after I came back from a winning season.

Listening to Frank's words of wisdom

One of my favorite moves

Doing a butterfly mid-air. Looks hard, doesn't it? But it's really pretty easy for me.

I love signing autographs for my fans.

skating is in my heart not my head.

Tonya or Nancy anymore. All they cared about was how well I could skate.

Frank and I huddled before my long program and tried to shut out the noise and the confusion and the crowd. But when I skated out onto the ice to take my starting pose, I suddenly felt like the world was on my side.

I tried to feel like a serious, mature, woman skater, standing out there in my ponytail and bare face, waiting for the music to start. I had never smiled much in programs before that year. But when I heard the crowd cheering, I couldn't help it — a huge smile spread from ear to ear.

The pressure was on, and I liked it. Correction: I *loved* it. This was the kind of attention and challenge I wanted. I didn't care about press conferences and tabloid TV. *This* was what made me feel alive. It was my first time at Worlds, and no one knew what to expect from me. I could surprise them.

I smiled all the way through my program. I went out there and did not one but *two* clean triple Lutzes. When I finished, the other American skaters — the men and pairs and dancers — screamed their approval. I'd done it! At my first world championships, I placed eighth. The American team had its two spots for the 1995 Worlds.

After being in the spotlight, I had a taste for more. Because of the attention I got at Worlds, I suddenly got a lot busier. I was invited to pro-am competitions, where professional and amateur skaters get to compete against one another. I skated at exhibitions and on tours. I was in demand!

That summer, Tom Collins, a producer and former skater, invited me to skate with his famous "Campbell's Soups Tour of World Figure Skating Champions." This was a big honor and a chance for me to make some money, which we badly needed. It was also a lot of fun.

My mom came with me. After all those years when we were too busy to spend more than five minutes at a time together, it felt so good to sit around our hotel room and tell each other stories. We talked about everything. Sometimes when I had a day off (and didn't have homework), we'd go shopping or just do nothing together. Having her all to myself seemed like a huge luxury. I was working all right, and sometimes I wished I could just lie out on the beach like other kids do during summer break. But I was happy. I really wouldn't have traded places with anyone.

We did seventy-six shows that summer, and I got to be on the same ice with all of my heroes. Brian Boitano! Oksana Baiul! Nancy Kerrigan! Figure-skating champions were everywhere.

How did it *feel* to be an Olympic champion? I still didn't know. I was too shy to ask them. By far the youngest on tour, I didn't know how to act around all those grown-ups yet.

One person who adopted me as his best friend was Tom Collins's brother Harris, who managed the tour and traveled on the bus with us from city to city. He always sat with me and made me laugh hysterically. I drove everyone else crazy by giggling all the time while they were trying to sleep. Harris and I became really great pals.

The tour was lots of fun. But training for the 1995 Nationals and Worlds was still my number-one priority. I had made sure that the American team had two spots for the upcoming Worlds. Now I had to make sure that one of them would be *mine*.

14
Frank

By now I'd been working for a solid year and a half with Frank Carroll. We really trusted each other. A skater's relationship with her coach is incredibly important. It can't work without absolute trust and honesty.

Many times I've looked Frank in the eye and asked, "What do I have to do now to take my skating to the next level?" He's always had the answer. All I have to do is listen and believe him.

Frank knows everything about skating, but he also has great insight about other things, like people. One summer, a skating teacher from Toronto named Lori Nichol brought a few of her students to Ice Castle for a couple of weeks. Her students weren't great skaters, but their programs were choreographed so beautifully and perfectly for them that they all *looked* like great skaters.

Frank noticed that and was impressed. So he went to Lori and asked her how she did it. He had a great feeling about her — she seemed like a wonderful person who really cared about her students. Pretty soon they were good friends, and he asked her to do some choreography for me.

Now Frank and Lori and I are like a family. When you have that support around you — in skating and in life — you can do so much more than you can do just by yourself.

That doesn't mean that life always goes smoothly for us. Frank and I do have fights. Maybe twice a year we'll have a big blowout. Sometimes it happens when there's pressure building toward a major event. Or when we've been working day and night on a new program and we're exhausted. I guess most of the time it's my fault. I can be pretty head-strong, if you haven't already guessed.

Frank and I are very close. I confide in him, and we joke around a lot. But we don't hang out after practice or go to movies together. We love and trust each other, but we're professionals. Our professional respect for each other is the key to our success.

Sometimes you need someone who won't tell you that you're great just because they love you. You need someone who will be honest, even if it means being *brutally* honest. That's what I get from Frank. (Of course, my family doesn't hold back on that, either. But more about them later.)

I've also learned from Frank what discipline really means. Now when I'm practicing my program, I never let a fall stop me from going on. If I'm not focused and working hard, he'll sit me down and have a very serious talk. He's a wonderful man, but when he gets mad, look out.

Some days I feel lazy. My life is jam-packed — every moment of it scheduled and planned weeks in advance — and sometimes I wish I could just be home watching TV. Or else my mind will wander — I'll be skating, but in my head I'm doing homework, conjugating French verbs!

Frank knows right away when that happens. In fact, he seems to know exactly what I'm thinking most of the time. It's amazing. He'll say, "Earth calling Michelle, hello!" and I'll come down from the clouds.

But I've also gotten to the point where the discipline comes from myself. Some days I'll just be really, really tired. I'll think, Okay, I'm only going to do the first part of my program. But once I get started, I don't stop. I go ahead and do the whole thing. No matter how tired I am, once I'm skating I remember exactly why it is that I'm there. Just a little bit more effort, I tell myself, and the rewards will be huge.

Focus and concentration are a big part of the work Frank and I do together, in practice and at competitions. We have a way of being magnets to each other. Before a competition, Frank's mind can pull mine into focus, as if by magnetic force.

We always look for a place backstage to get away from everyone else. We look for a place where there are no TV cameras, no fans, no other competitors.

Once Frank and I are alone, we get very serious. I do warm-up exercises and stretches. They're very important. It's cold out there on the ice. If your muscles aren't warm they could easily cramp up.

We do floor work, which means I practice jumps in my sneakers. Then I close my eyes and visualize my program. Sometimes I even see myself falling! But just like in practice, I push my mind to keep on going through the entire program. Frank reminds me to have "tunnel vision." That means staying focused on my goal, seeing only what I want to do on the ice, and putting blinders on to everything else.

In a competition, the skaters are divided into groups of five or six. After each group finishes, the next group gets a short warm-up. After that, if you're the last in your group, you could have a long wait, so you have to keep your muscles warm.

When it's time, Frank and I get up and make our way to the ice. By now, we've got our tunnel vision going. Our minds have pushed away all the people and have zoned in on our goal — to skate my very best.

You can see how serious I am right before I skate. I never smile. Frank will give me one last word of advice before I take my starting position. It'll be the thing I need most to remember right then. Usually it's some kind of reminder to let myself skate free.

When I was little, I had all kinds of rituals. I thought I had to have them (like my dirty skates) or else I wouldn't do well. But when I started working with Frank, I realized those rituals were going nowhere, and I dropped most of them.

I still do have a few little habits, though. I have a little teddy-bear backpack that always comes with me to competitions. He's very cute, but he's also very practical! You can carry little things in his back. Sometimes while I'm loosening up my muscles, Frank loosens up my mind by making Mr. Bear do perfect triple Lutzes.

And I never take off the necklace my grandmother gave me. You'll see it next time you see me on TV sitting in the "Kiss and Cry" area (that's what everyone calls the place where we wait for our scores with our coaches).

Frank has suffered through my rituals. I'll never forget the time he had to polish my skates in Junior Nationals. It says a lot about him that he was willing to do that. Now I know that having Frank on my side is more important than having rituals. Our trust in each other can do so much more.

15

The Birmingham Year

I love to travel. Part of the excitement of a competition is getting to go to a place I've never been before. My parents and I always try to take little side trips when we're in a new country.

In Beijing, China, for instance, I got to walk on the Great Wall. That was exciting, but it got a little too exciting when a camel nearly kicked me off the wall!

I also like to try the local food. In China, I ate real Chinese food (almost as good as my dad's). In France, I ate real crepes. Someday I'd like to go to Belgium and have one of my all-time favorite foods — Belgian waffles (we have them just about every Sunday that we're home). And next time I'm in Japan, maybe I'll have green-tea ice cream and sushi (the kind with *cooked* fish, please!).

I always remember a competition by the city it's in. The San Jose Nationals. The Paris Skate International. The St. Petersburg Centennial on Ice. For me, the 1994–95 season will always be the Birmingham year.

After the 1994 Worlds in Japan, Nancy Kerrigan turned professional and Tonya Harding was no longer a member of the USFSA. That left me and Nicole Bobek as the two top American skaters.

Nicole had been having some troubles lately. So everybody seemed to be looking at me as the favorite to win the 1995 Nationals, which would be held in Providence, Rhode Island. And they also saw me as America's best hope at the Worlds in Birmingham, England.

All season long, people said my skating was really improving. They kept calling me the "favorite." It was hard to believe that at the age of fourteen that could be true. The Tonya-Nancy story had brought new attention to women's skating, and there were more skating fans than ever. I did all kinds of interviews and appearances. By the time Nationals rolled around, I'd heard that I was the "favorite" so many times that I almost believed it.

It was especially fun to be in Providence because Karen was there, too, skating in her first Senior Nationals. All the reporters thought that the "Kwan sisters" were an interesting story. We did all kinds of interviews together on TV and for newspapers and magazines. People wanted to know if we ever got jealous of each other. We always answered honestly, like Shep told us to, and the answer was always "no." Being together at Nationals just made it all so much more fun.

Having Karen in Providence was great, and I loved my programs. Frank, Lori, and I had worked hard on them. I was excited to get out there and skate them. But I wasn't thrilled about this "favorite" business.

In the short program, I bobbled my triple-Lutz/double-toe combination and was in third place going into the freeskate. That made people stop talking pretty quickly. Nicole, Tonia Kwiatkowski, and I were neck-and-neck in the top three. Nicole was looking very good, so suddenly everyone was buzzing about *her*.

I was the last skater in the last group for the long program. After the warm-up, I had to wait forty-five minutes before taking the ice. I spent the whole time keeping my muscles warm and trying to stay relaxed and focused with Frank.

Nicole skated right before me. She skated well in her program, but not perfectly. There was still a little room for me.

Finally it was my turn. I could have used another warm-up. Even so, everything went great for the first three and a half minutes. My first triple Lutz was clean. My triple flip — the next hardest jump for me — was good. At the end of the program, I had only one jump left, my second triple Lutz.

Going into it, I could tell I didn't have enough speed. Before I even took off into the air I knew I would fall. And sure enough, I crashed down right onto my hip. Nicole ended up with the gold, proving that everyone had been wrong to underestimate her, and I got the silver.

Once again, I'd had a chance to do my best at Nationals. Once again, the triple Lutz did me in. But because of my second-place finish, I was still going to the world championships in Birmingham.

We took a new approach in Birmingham. Frank decided to make both my programs harder! He replaced some of the jumps that were easier for me with ones that were more difficult. My long program had seven triples. Nobody there had harder programs than mine.

In the short program, I followed Surya Bonaly, whom I'd looked up to so much when I first went to Ice Castle. I still wasn't used to skating with all the top skaters. It was still so exciting to me.

My nerves didn't show, though. I skated my program perfectly. I didn't make a single mistake. But when my scores came up they were lower than everyone expected.

In the Kiss and Cry I turned to Frank and asked, "Should my scores be so low?" I was seriously confused. I'd never skated better. Frank explained that, to the judges, I was still a kid and that might have caused them to give me lower marks.

Going into the long program I was in fifth place. Lu Chen, Surya, and Nicole were all above me.

None of that really mattered to me, though. I was at Worlds and I was determined to do my best. I loved my long program. I wasn't going to let any single jump or any score ruin my fun.

Right before I went out for the freeskate, Frank said, "Sparkle!"

Standing in the middle of the ice, looking out and waiting for my music, all of a sudden that's exactly what the world was doing in my eyes. Sparkling!

I flew through every jump and every spin. I landed cleanly time after time after time. . . . I heard the crowd roaring and I spun like a top. I had speed going into my first triple Lutz and speed coming out of it. All my troubles with triple Lutzes seemed like a distant memory. My second triple Lutz was such a snap that I tacked on a double toe-loop to make it a combination.

After all my jumps were behind me, I did a spread eagle. As I arced around the ice, I could see the crowd standing, waving American flags . . . and *sparkling*. I was so happy. I started smiling and crying at the same time.

When it was over, I just lost it. The tears poured out of my eyes. I had never skated better in my life, and I was crying like a baby. There was so much I loved about skating — the challenge, the competition, the feeling of flying.

I was so happy after that skate that the

scores didn't matter at all. In the end, although I was the only one to skate two flawless programs, I came in fourth. Lu Chen won, Surya got the silver, and Nicole got the bronze.

After things had settled down and my head felt clear, I did some serious thinking. I realized that I could keep on being the kind of skater I was — athletic, a good jumper . . . a kid. But if I did, I couldn't hope to do any better than I had done that night. I'd never become the kind of skater I'd always dreamed of being — a skater like Brian Boitano, Peggy Fleming, Dorothy Hamill. . . .

I knew I needed to change. As a kid skater, I'd gone as far as I could. Now I needed to find Michelle, the Lady skater — the artist. For once, I didn't need Frank to tell me what to do next. I knew.

16

Growing Up

If there's one thing I know about life, it's that everything is changing all the time. It might seem sometimes like you'll *never* be treated like a grown-up. But the great thing about being young is that you don't stay the same for long. If you don't like being fourteen, don't worry. In a year you'll turn fifteen, like I did in 1995.

After Birmingham, people had this picture of me in their heads. I was the cute, ponytailed kid who could jump like a bean. As far as they knew, that's all I'd ever be.

People wondered what would happen to me when my body started changing. A lot of people worried that my career would crash. That my hips would get bigger and I'd topple over.

That I wouldn't be able to get off the ground or something.

Luckily I don't pay much attention to what "most people" say. The people I listen to carefully are my family, my coach, my manager, my choreographer, my close friends, and other skaters I admire. Most of all, I listen to my heart. It's hard enough just to grow up — without listening to what the whole world is saying about you.

After Birmingham, I knew that I needed to do more than make my skating better technically. I needed to find a whole new *dimension* to my skating. I told Frank and Lori that I wanted to become a more "artistic" skater. I said I was ready to do something drastically different from the programs I'd done before. And I really, really did not want to be *cute* anymore!

The fact was that certain natural changes *were* happening to me, and I couldn't stop them even if I wanted to. During the summer after Birmingham I grew a couple of inches. My body did start to change. I guess that in September the change seemed sudden to people who hadn't seen me for a while. But I'd been growing and adapting to changes in my body my entire life. I handled it pretty well, I think. In fact, I kind of liked it.

Growing up doesn't just happen to your body. It happens to your emotions and your mind, too. I wanted to take a new approach to my skating partly because I knew I needed to if I was going to be successful. But I also *had* to. My feelings were getting more complicated, and I wanted to show those feelings in my skating.

Frank and Lori had the same idea. They'd probably seen it long before I did. So we all agreed to focus on the artistic side of my program that year. We were excited. It was a great challenge we could all sink our teeth into.

Lori says her job is to bring out the beauty in me when I'm skating. It's not an easy job. Lori has to know everything about what the judges require and everything about skating. But she also has to know me — both my skating and my heart.

I mentioned earlier how the really great skaters are both athletes and artists. It may sound like these go together like ice cream and pie, but the truth is there's a lot of tension between them. On the one hand, you need incredible precision and athleticism for the jumps and other technical parts of your program. On the other, you want to find an open, flowing way to express what the music and skating mean to you. These are two very different states of mind. Blending them so they belong together is what makes figure skating such an unusual and difficult sport.

Lori is really good at explaining this and trying to make the two blend. We develop three programs every year — my long program, my short program, and another program that I use for exhibitions and the special competitions outside the regular Olympic-style circuit.

You'd be amazed at the amount of work Lori puts into my programs. Before she can even get started on the choreography, she has to spend a long time listening to all kinds of music, trying to find the perfect piece. To start with, it must be something that can be skated to. That means it has to have the right kind of rhythm and pace and emotion.

But most of all, it should be a piece of music that reminds her of me. (Or *pieces* of music — lots of times we edit different things together.) It should express some feeling about where I am in that particular moment of my constantly changing life.

Sometimes it takes us a while to find something we can all agree on. After Birmingham, Lori and Frank played some music for me that they both liked. I listened to it, but it didn't do anything for me. I knew I couldn't skate to it.

At first they were a little upset. They'd looked so long for this music, and they both liked it. They'd even worked out some of the choreography. But it's a good thing I spoke up. If I hadn't, Frank never would have thought of "Salome."

"Salome" is a music-drama by the German composer Richard Strauss. He adapted the story from the New Testament. In the Bible, Salome does her dance of the seven veils for Herod Antipas, who in return gives her the head of John the Baptist on a platter. Yikes!

Okay, I admit I was a little shocked when I heard the whole story. But I liked it because it was definitely not a *cute* story. It's true that the character wasn't exactly *me*. But I wanted to do something dramatic, something that would force me to find a more mature Michelle. Salome seemed right. I loved the idea of acting a role while I skated.

When she had created a piece, she came to Lake Arrowhead. She taught me the choreography, and we worked out the kinks together. Sometimes the moves she comes up with are

93

more comfortable for her than for me to do. So we make adjustments until the program suits my body and my skating. Frank, of course, has a lot to say about it, too.

Once the choreography was set, I had to learn it so well that I could skate it without thinking about what came next. And then I had to *become* Salome.

Something amazing happened to me when I got to that point. The music and the character seemed to transform me. I was still fifteen and just a kid, but Salome started to bring out another more mature person. Off the ice I wasn't really so different, just a little taller and a little rounder here and there. But on the ice, I had grown up.

The first time I skated Salome in public was in October at the 1995 Skate America in Detroit, Michigan. I didn't know what people would think. Maybe they'd think I was forcing myself to act older than I really was. The story of Salome is pretty heavy. It was nothing like the light and bouncy programs I'd done before.

Most people hadn't seen me for a while. And I guess I did look pretty different. The year before, Skate America had taken place on Halloween — Karen and I went out trick-ortreating as Fred Flintstone and Barney Rubble. But this year, I showed up as Salome.

It was the first time anyone had seen me in makeup. The ponytail was gone. The plain face was gone. My lips were red. My hair was piled high. My costume was sophisticated and elegant. I was taller. I was more confident. People said they hardly recognized me. Is that *Michelle?*

Maybe I *was* pretending to be older than my age. But I approached Skate America more as a performance than as a competition. And I'd never had so much fun!

It seemed like we were on the right track. At Skate America I beat Lu Chen, who had just beaten me and everyone else at Birmingham to become world champion. But now that I had successfully become Salome, the question remained: Could I become a champion?

17

On Top of the World

Every time I competed that season leading up to the 1996 Nationals, I grew more comfortable as Salome. We went to a lot more competitions that year than we had the year before. Each time, Frank and I worked hard to polish every single line so that it became a *whole* program, not just a lot of jumps and spins one after the other.

By the time we got to San Jose for Nationals, I had competed as Salome so often that I didn't have time to get nervous. It seemed like just another day to me.

The first three times I'd been to Nationals, everyone had thought of me as a little kid. In those days, I didn't feel like I belonged with the big kids — with the older, more experienced women skaters. I loved being there with them; it was like a dream come true. But I didn't feel like an equal to the others. It always seemed possible that I might skate my very best at Nationals, but I never really believed my best would be good enough.

Well, in 1996 I finally felt like I belonged at Nationals. It was so great to be able to say to myself, at last, If I skate my best, I know I'll win. That's when I felt as if I'd really arrived at the top level of skating.

When I stepped on the ice in San Jose, I knew that the championship could be mine. It didn't do any good to be modest about it. It was just the truth. If I did my best, the gold medal was in my reach.

And my best was exactly what I did. Luckily I didn't trip over any Lutzes or make any dumb mistakes. I skated the program I'd grown into all year. My best *was* good enough — good enough for the gold.

After I skated my program, I got to watch Karen skate her best, too. She had such a unique and beautiful presence on the ice that she finished in fifth place, ahead of lots of other skaters who had more triple jumps.

Karen's accomplishment really did seem as thrilling as mine. We were so happy for each other. Karen's success made my night feel

97

complete. And you wouldn't believe how proud my mom and dad were.

After all those second-place medals, I was finally standing there on the podium with a gold medal around my neck. I stood up there smiling and weeping at the same time, as usual. I may still have had my teddy-bear backpack, and I would always be my mother's "baby," but from then on I would never be a "kid" skater again.

Even though I'd won Nationals, I wasn't considered the favorite to win Worlds in Edmonton, Canada. I was just *one* of the favorites. A lot of great skaters were there, including Lu Chen, the defending champion, and Midori Ito, another former world champion.

But, favorite or not, I was at my favorite competition. And what I felt at Nationals, I felt even more strongly at Edmonton — that *my* best could be *the* best.

After my short program — a flamenco-style routine — I was in first place, so things were looking good. But the freeskate counts for much more, so the competition was still anybody's to win.

Lu seemed to be as confident as I was. She

skated a great long program. Frank and I were in the flower girls' (they're the girls who pick up the flowers that are thrown on the ice) dressing room backstage when we heard her scores. She got two 6.0's for artistic expression! Those were perfect scores. No woman had ever gotten 6.0's at Worlds, at least not that anyone could remember.

Now I was panicked. "How can I beat that?" I asked Frank.

"There's still a little bit of room," Frank answered — because after the 6.0's, the announcer read a couple of 5.8's.

Frank was right. There was a little opening for me after all. If I got 5.9's where Lu got 5.8's, I could sneak through.

I went out on the ice and felt that great surge of energy that I've always felt at Worlds, and that I'd been feeling all season long. My music started. Now I wasn't the little kid they'd patted on the head last year. I was Salome. I was dynamite.

My program was going perfectly. As I came to the close, I hadn't made any mistakes. But Lu hadn't made any big mistakes, either. So I thought: I've got to do something more to push ahead of her. With a second or two to go in the program, I had only a double Axel left.

99

In the blink of an eye, I decided to turn that
Axel into a triple toe-loop. That would give
me one more triple jump than Lu.

I got up a little extra speed, took a breath,
and took off into the jump. I landed it cleanly.
Then I saw that the audience was coming to
their feet. I saw those wonderful American
flags waving. I'd done it!

I *tried* not to cry. I hit myself on the head, as
if to wake myself up from a dream. But that
must have knocked the tears loose, because
they came tumbling out. My emotions overwhelmed me.

The judges gave me two 6.0's, too. It was
very close, but most of them ranked me ahead
of Lu. I was the gold medalist. Todd Eldredge
had also won a gold in the men's competition,
so it was the first American sweep at Worlds
since Debi Thomas and Brian Boitano won in
1986. I had something in common with Brian,
my hero!

What a year. First I became wicked Salome,
who did her dance in order to have someone's
head delivered to her on a platter. And then I
became the world champion. You could even
say I had become famous.

People asked if it surprised me. In a weird

way, no. I mean, one part of me just couldn't believe that I was at the top of the podium. Yet at the same time, it seemed logical. After all, I'd been climbing that podium step by step for the past three years.

18
Life at the Top

Now that I'd reached the top, the requests for interviews and appearances went through the roof. I learned early on from Shep that the best thing when you're talking to the press is just to tell the truth. That way you can be yourself around them and you'll never get caught in a lie. But I also had to learn how to tell the same stories over and over again as if I'd never told them before.

I'm a naturally open person, so I'd find myself answering anything anybody asked me without thinking about it first. I'd just open my mouth and talk, even on television, like I did on the David Letterman show. Sometimes I'd rewind what I had said and think, That was so stupid! But it was too late to change it.

I was invited to every skating exhibition.

People wanted me to make special appearances all over the place. I did all kinds of TV shows. I was even invited to visit President Clinton in the White House. I would have loved to have gone, but I didn't have enough time! "Sorry, Mr. President. Can't make it."

I got thousands of fan letters and autograph requests. Kids sent me presents. I got so many stuffed animals you wouldn't believe it. Little girls would send them to me or throw them onto the ice, usually with little stickers where they'd written their names and addresses. It was so sweet! I always wrote back and sent a picture. I couldn't believe how nice all the fans were.

I developed a Christmas card list, too. Everyone who'd supported me — sportswriters, friends, fellow skaters: They were all on it.

Meanwhile, I still had to study hard so my grades wouldn't slip. It seemed like the tutor was always at my house. Between practices, engagements, and interviews, my head was buried in a book. Even though I get carsick really easily, I still had to study on my way to practice and photo shoots and interviews. It was the only spare time I had!

At Ice Castle, my friends didn't act differently toward me. But whenever new young skaters came to the rink, I'd see them pointing at me and hear them saying in a whisper, "That's Michelle Kwan." They looked up to me the way I had looked up to Lu Chen, Nancy Kerrigan, and Kristi Yamaguchi when I was little. It was really neat to think I might inspire a new young skater.

I also had to get used to hearing people talk about me all the time. Wherever I'd go it seemed that people were having meetings to discuss where I should go next, when they could make an appointment to make an appointment, or how I felt about the weather. Thank goodness for Shep! Reporters were always asking him, Frank, and my family, "How does she feel, now that she's a champion?"

When I told people that I wasn't really surprised to become world champion, the answer maybe sounded a little arrogant. But the fact was that I wasn't surprised. That's not the word for it. Excited, overwhelmed, happy: yes. But ever since I was seven, I had imagined myself as a championship skater.

Whenever I'd asked myself, Can this really happen to me? an inner voice had always answered *yes*. I'd been working for it my whole life. So *surprise* is not really the right word.

And when the day came for me to lose it, I

wouldn't be surprised then, either. Right now, I was the youngest American world champion ever and the third-youngest world champion period. I felt incredibly lucky to have achieved so much at such a young age.

After I won, everything was happening so fast that it made my head spin. I began to wonder if I'd ever have a chance to enjoy it. My dad always says, "There's a good and a bad side to everything in life." The only bad thing about winning is that someday you have to lose what you've won. I already knew that I couldn't be world champion forever. I just wished I could stop everything and look at it all, as if it were a picture, so I could appreciate what had happened.

I would never again be the kid skater I had been just one year earlier, when no one but me and the people who knew me had any idea that I was capable of becoming Salome. But somewhere out there there was another little kid with a ponytail and no makeup. She had her own dreams and was working as hard as I had. Nobody paid much attention to Tara Lipinski at Worlds that year. She was twenty-third after the short program, fifteenth overall. But she knew what she could do. And it probably didn't surprise her when she did it, either.

19

Coming Back to Earth

When I look back on my life, I have to say that the long process of *becoming* world champion was the most fun I've had. Every time I stepped on the ice, I was so excited that I never thought of fear. I loved to skate — to feel like I was flying. It seemed that there was nowhere to go but up.

But *being* world champ? Wow. That was something else altogether. I was standing up there with a gold medal, and the view was great. There was only one problem: Where do you fly from there?

It's not that I felt like a different person. I didn't. But I definitely was in a different place with a new outlook. Now there was nothing around me but sky, for miles and miles. And down below, earth.

During the summer after my championship season I went out on Tom Collins's Campbell's Soups Tour. I was really looking forward
to that. You'd think touring seventy-six cities
in three months would be exhausting, but in
reality it was a nice break from the regular season with all its pressures and competitions.

On tour, I'd have to try and catch up with
the schoolwork I'd fallen behind on. But I'd
get to have some fun, too. So many of the
skaters I'd admired for so long had become my
good friends. Brian Boitano, Elvis Stojko, Jenni
Meno, Todd Sand . . . on and on.

The guys could help the girls with their
triple Axels. On the bus, we'd all watch
movies.(Well, *they'd* watch movies; I'd try to
do my homework.) Mom would come with
me, as always, and we'd talk all the time and go
shopping when we had the chance.

I always look forward to spending the summer with Mom on tour, just the two of us. We
always feel so happy and comfortable when
we're alone together. We're a perfect match.
We share all our secrets and laugh and act silly
like a couple of girlfriends. And of course she
takes care of me, too. She makes sure that
when I'm not working hard, being myself, or
having fun, that I'm sleeping and eating well.

107

Frank doesn't come with me on tour, so I count on Mom for all kinds of advice — even skating advice.

Something else I loved about going on tour was getting to spend time with my buddy Harris Collins. Everyone on the tour knew that I was best friends with him. They knew that if they saw Harris, Michelle couldn't be far behind. He was forty-nine, which was a lot older than me, but that never mattered. We both acted like kids.

None of the other skaters treated me differently now that I was world champion. To most people I was still "Shelley," as they call me on tour. A lot of them had been world champions, too. I was still like everyone's kid sister.

Skating in a show is a lot different from skating in a competition. First of all, the arena is dark, except for a spotlight on the skater. That's kind of neat, but hard to get used to. In a competition, the arena is brightly lit and you can make eye contact with the judges. They get to see a bit of your personality that way. But on tour, you can't see the audience at all. In fact, you can only see a couple of feet ahead of you.

Most skaters use programs on tour that

aren't as challenging as their regular long programs. But not all. Brian Boitano, for one, is
amazing. He goes out there each night and
puts every ounce of himself into his program.
You can see that for him skating itself is the
greatest thrill and the highest honor — greater
and higher than all the medals he has won.

I wanted to skate all-out like that, too. I
knew I couldn't let up just because I had a
couple gold medals. I had just won Worlds, but
I was already thinking about the next season.
What were my new goals? The answer was
fuzzy . . . not to lose? What kind of goal was
that?

I decided that the thing to do was simply to
work harder than I'd ever worked before. To
not let up for a minute. "Work *harder*, be yourself, and have fun" was my new motto.

It should have been my happiest summer,
but I was feeling confused about my goals.
Keeping the championship was my new objec-
tive, not getting it. Suddenly I felt more serious than I had before. Having fun got to be
hard — especially when we lost Harris Collins.

It was June 1, 1996. We were in Chicago, at
the United Center, and Harris had just told us
that there were five minutes before the start of

the show. He walked past the dressing room. Then we heard screaming — it was Harris.

None of us knew exactly what had happened, but one of the skaters had seen Harris fall. The show was about to start, and we had to go on the ice to be introduced. It was awful. "What happened to Harris?" we all asked. All we knew was that he had been taken to the hospital. I was crying when the announcer introduced me, tears streaming down my face as I skated out into the bright spotlight.

Since we hadn't heard anything from the hospital, I assumed Harris was okay. I skated my program and held myself together. The sound of the audience cheering helped to make me feel better. No news, I thought, was good news.

I didn't find out what happened until that night, when Mom and I were on our way to a special engagement I had to do in Florida. Harris had died of a heart attack. I suddenly realized how *young* forty-nine years old was. He was gone. One minute he had been okay. The next minute . . . where was he?

I was on an airplane when I heard the news. Now all my thoughts about flying toward goals and flying on the ice seemed much less important than the questions, Where was Harris? What had happened? *Why?*

I'd lost other important people in my life — Virginia Fratianne died the year before, and Mr. Probst from Ice Castle the year before that. But this was the first time someone so close to me — right *there* — was suddenly taken away.

I wrote a poem for Harris that night. I don't know if it's a good poem or not. But it says how I felt.

What is death?
Death is a question to ask.
There is no answer.
It is impossible.
We shall all leave earth, but it is not death.
Every day we disintegrate.
Bit by bit we leave the face of the earth.
Losing the touch of the ground.
Floating to what will become.
But-it-is-no-death.

111

20

Clipped Wings

No matter how much we missed Harris, the tour had to go on. I still think about him all the time. But every day it got a little bit more possible to get on the bus without him, to start the show on time without him, even to laugh without him. I don't know how it got easier. I just know that, amazingly, it did.

I'm sure it helped to be so busy. We were always on our way to a new place. There were always fans outside the stage door waiting for autographs. In every city, there were reporters who wanted to ask us questions. And my mom was always there to talk through things with me and to make me feel better.

The fans probably helped me as much as anything. Every night when the announcer introduced me and I skated out onto the ice, I heard this warm, wonderful sound from the audience. It made me forget everything . . . except that I wanted to skate for them. While I was on the ice, I was happy. Nothing else mattered.

Sometimes we skaters took shopping excursions and side trips. When we were in Alaska, Lloyd Eisler and Todd Eldredge organized a fishing trip. Lots of the skaters were planning to go, but when the day arrived, it was raining. Everyone dropped out except Todd, Lloyd, and me.

My dad and I fish all the time on Lake Arrowhead, and I missed it. I missed Dad, too. The rain didn't matter to me. I wanted to get out onto the water and try to have that feeling Dad and I have when we're together.

The guys and I huddled on the boat in the rain, and waited for a bite. Finally I felt a tug on my line. And then a tug-of-war. I knew that if I asked Todd and Lloyd to help me reel it in they'd tease me for the rest of the tour. So I dug in and didn't give up. The fish seemed just as intent on pulling me into the water as I was on pulling it out. Todd and Lloyd thought it was hysterical. But in the end I won what turned out to be a twenty-five-pound salmon.

By July the tour was over. Soon I was back

home fishing with Dad again. But things had changed there, too. We had moved into our own house in Lake Arrowhead the December before — a place of our own again, at last. It wasn't huge, but it seemed a lot bigger than the cabin. Big, but kind of empty. Ron had been away at college a few years, so I was used to that. But this year Karen went away, too — a long way away to Boston University.

It was just me and my parents now. I'd run into the house after practice and want to tell Karen something, but she wasn't there. It was weird. I'd wake up in the morning and want to tell her my dreams. But I couldn't, unless I called her on the telephone. It seemed so quiet at home.

Luckily I have a great relationship with my parents. We tell each other everything. I don't think I've ever lied to them — not seriously enough for me to remember it. Anyway, they'd see right through me if I tried.

My parents expect a lot from all of us kids. They've always set down very clear guidelines. They always tell us what's right and wrong.

I don't know what they'd do if I did anything seriously wrong. My parents trust us to be good. They're not into punishment. They always say, "If you follow our guidelines, then

114

we're good parents. If you don't, then we're bad parents."

If you spend a few minutes with my dad, he'll be happy to spell out the guidelines for you, too. Dad is a kind of philosopher. Last year he retired from the phone company and turned the management of the restaurant over to someone else. So he's suddenly got a lot of time to think and to talk.

And I actually listen to him. I think lots of kids don't pay attention to their parents' advice. But I live by my parents' wisdom. I really do. I don't always have time to learn from my own mistakes, so I need to learn from theirs.

I think the reason a lot of kids don't believe what their parents tell them is that they don't believe that bad things can happen to them. They don't realize that bad things haven't happened to them *because* their parents have taken care of them.

My parents' philosophies have helped me at every stage of my life. If you haven't noticed that as I've been telling my story, you've missed something! Every day my life gets a little more complicated, or something totally new happens, and I rely on Mom and Dad to help me make sense of it.

I'm not saying I agree with *everything* my

parents say. Or that you can fix every problem with a word of advice. Some problems you really do need to figure out by yourself. I have my own mind and a few of my own philosophies, too. But I always listen very carefully to what they say and share my own thoughts with them. I'm really grateful that *they're* good listeners, too.

Maybe the biggest lesson I've learned from my parents is that *regret* is a terrible word. It's the number-one thing to avoid in life. I agree with that. When you have an opportunity, you have to take it. You can't let yourself be lazy or afraid, or else you'll end up looking back, saying, "If only I had worked harder, I could have made it." But at the same time, you shouldn't do anything unless your heart is in it.

You have to be careful. After Edmonton, I kept thinking about that word *regret*. All I could think to do to avoid regret was to work as hard as I could. I trained hard and competed hard. As the new season started, I took gold medals in the first two competitions.

But something was missing. I didn't know what it was yet. For the first time in my life, I wasn't happy just to be on the ice. It's weird, but I felt like my wings had been clipped. Maybe it was because I was at the top of the world, and for a moment I didn't have new goals to fly toward.

Fixing my problem wasn't simple. It turned out that I'd have to experience some disappointment first. I'd need some advice from my parents, too, but it wouldn't be enough on its own.

My father is always willing to share his opinions, and it's funny how he knows he's not always right. Lots of times, for instance, he gets lost driving to a competition. I'm always teasing him about it. Luckily he takes the teasing well.

We'll go fishing sometimes, and he'll philosophize for an hour. I'll think, My dad really knows a lot about life (except for the things I disagree with, of course). Then, at the end of the hour, he'll sum up by saying, "But I'm just a simple man. I could be wrong."

And with that little last sentence, he makes sure he's always right.

21

My Favorite Things

With all this talk about skating and regret and flying and training and touring, I don't want to give the impression that that's all there is to my life. It's true that most of my days are completely scheduled and that one of my favorite pastimes is napping. But I do manage to have a little plain, old, regular fun, too. Everyone needs a break!

I have to admit that one of my favorite things to do is shop. I'm not interested in buying things that you can't use, like knickknacks or fancy toys. I specialize in clothes, with the occasional raid into the makeup department and the music racks.

I never wore anything but hand-me-downs until I was thirteen years old — fourth generation hand-me-downs at that. Now that I can afford to buy new clothes, I take shopping pretty seriously. But carefully, too. I'm a bargain hunter. Generally speaking, I buy things on sale or else I don't buy them at all. And when I do buy a nice sweater or dress, I treat it with care.

One of my dad's favorite philosophies is, "It's good to be a success and to be able to afford hundred-dollar shoes. As long as you won't mind going back to twenty-dollar shoes if you have to." He means that I shouldn't get too caught up in having money, and he's right. But I prefer to interpret it this way: "It's better to pay twenty dollars for hundred-dollar shoes."

Most of my life I've done without expensive things and have been quite happy, so long as I could skate. No matter how much I love shopping now, I'd always make the same choice — skates over shoes, every day of the week. In the meantime, I like to think that I have a healthy teenage appetite for fashion.

After I won at Worlds, the only people who seemed to treat me any differently were the ones who work in stores. It's odd. I guess because I'm young, salespeople sometimes act rudely to me, assuming I don't have any money to buy things. But as soon as someone tells them I'm "Michelle Kwan," they act differently — they treat me like a celebrity. That seems wrong to me, and it makes me mad. My friends and I don't buy anything when we get that kind of treatment.

Lots of times people in stores and on the street recognize me and want my autograph. That's fun, but it's hard to get used to. The weirdest thing is when I go to some event where there are famous people — athletes and movie stars. I'll be staring at *them*, and then they'll come over to *me* and say, "Michelle Kwan! I'm so happy to meet you!" I just about die when that happens.

Most of the people I'm close to, outside of my family, aren't movie stars. A lot of them are skaters, but I have friends in the real world, too. I still keep in touch with my best friend from Rancho Palos Verdes. We don't see each other much, but we're pen pals.

Last summer one of my friends came with Mom, Karen, and me on my first-ever real vacation — four days in the Cayman Islands. We swam with the stingrays, watched out for sharks (you know how I feel about them!), laid out on the beach, shopped (of course), went Jet Skiing, and talked till we dropped.

My friends and I go shopping all the time and go to movies and to amusement parks.

We've been to Space Mountain at Disneyland. I love rides. My favorite is the Colossus at Magic Mountain. It has a drop that makes you lose everything. It's like, "Oh, my god, I can't breathe!"

One of my all-time favorite adventures was a whitewater rafting trip I took with some of the skaters on tour a couple summers ago. I love swimming and I love rides, so white-water rafting is the perfect thing for me. And there are definitely no sharks in river rapids! It was weird. While we were rafting, it was so scary that I kept wishing it would end. But when it was over I kept wishing it would happen all over again!

I like adventure in general. I love going to all kinds of movies, but I especially like the action-adventure ones. I have too many favorite movies to list them here. But some of my favorite movie stars are Brad Pitt, Harrison Ford, Leonardo Di Caprio, and Jim Carrey.

Every now and then someone makes a movie about skating. There's an old one called *Ice Castles*, which is about a girl who keeps on skating even after she goes blind. A more recent one, *The Cutting Edge*, is about a snotty girl who becomes pairs-partners with a hockey player. I'll confess I've seen them about a million times. But I have to say they're pretty un-realistic. Then again, if I went blind, I'm pretty sure I'd find a way to keep skating, too.

I have lots of favorite musicians. I like melodic music that some of my friends think is boring. My favorites right now are Natalie Merchant, Tracy Chapman, Tori Amos, Jewel, and Celine Dion. I also like Sting's song "Fields of Gold." I've always wanted Brian Boitano to skate to that. I like songs that have meaning to them. I listen to music a lot in the car, and head-banger music makes me crazy. I don't need loud music to give me a headache while I'm driving.

I love to drive. But I've never been more ner-vous — not at Worlds, not at Nationals, not anywhere — than when I took my driving test. I was perspiring from every pore. My hands were literally shaking on the wheel. I can stand in front of a panel of nine judges without the slightest knee-wobble, but this one examiner threw me into a panic.

Let me tell you, a three-point turn is *nothing* like a triple Lutz. If I don't have a lot of speed going into a jump like that, I'll fail for sure. My three-point turn, in contrast, suffered from a little bit *too much* speed, at the wrong mo-ment. I flunked the test. But a couple of weeks later, I got another chance with a different examiner and aced it.

I have my own car — a Jeep Grand Cherokee. But I don't get to drive it many places, except to the rink and back. Most of my time off from the rink is taken up by schoolwork.

I have a full course load every year. This year I'm taking English, French, calculus, among other subjects. Because I get pulled away by competitions during the regular school year, I don't get time off for summer break. And although my tutor is very smart, she doesn't know the meaning of "weekend." She's at my house every day, including Sundays.

I've tried to work as hard at school as I have at skating (I manage to maintain a B+ average) because I have another dream, which I haven't mentioned yet: I want to go to Harvard.

I'm not sure what I'd major in if I got in. All I know is that if I close my eyes, I can see myself there, rushing to my next class. When I visited, I loved the feeling of the campus and the Ivy League tradition, not to mention the fact that Karen's nearby, at Boston University.

I read a lot for my homework, and I'm always on the lookout for inspirational quotes, which I copy into my diary. For instance, this

123

quote from *Walden* (which I read for English) by Henry David Thoreau:

However mean your life is, meet it and live it; do not shun it and call it hard names. It is not so bad as you are. It looks poorest when you are richest. The fault-finder will find faults even in paradise.

My diary is my buddy. I write everything down in there. But I'm not good at hiding it. It's always popping up in strange places around the house, like in the middle of the kitchen table. I'll see it and scream, "Aaagh! What's it doing *there*?!"

Luckily it's a very small book and I have to use tiny handwriting. I don't think anyone could read it anyway.

I love poetry, too. Karen and I both like writing poetry. That's something else I'd like to do when I have more time.

Come to think of it, there are a lot of things I don't have time for . . . not yet, anyway. Dating is another. My mother gave me a pretty ring, which only fits on my wedding finger. Sometimes people actually ask me if I'm engaged! Aren't I too young to be engaged? I'm only seventeen!

I've always thought that I'd get married by twenty-six and have kids by the time I'm twenty-eight. But who knows?

I do like to try to picture it, though. For instance, if it were up to me I think I'd like to have two little boys. I hope they won't want to be skaters (the skating mom's life is tough!), but if they do, I won't stop them. It's good for kids to have something to do outside of school — something they don't need to be pushed into doing, something they love.

But right now, I don't have much time to meet guys who aren't preoccupied with quadruple toe-loops, let alone someone I could actually fall in love with. But if Brad Pitt is interested, then that's another story. . . .

I'm too tired to stay out late anyway. No one has to give *me* a curfew. Not my parents, not Frank. If I didn't take a couple naps a day and go to bed early, I'd be a wreck. But I don't mind. I don't feel like I'm missing anything, honestly.

Wait — of course I'm missing something. I know that there are other ways to live life. But I've thought hard about it, and this is the life I want to lead right now. I don't know if it's perfect, but it's mine.

125

Wherever I go, I look at people and I try to imagine their lives. I always wonder: Are they happy? Was my driving examiner happy? Is the guy I passed on the street happy, or is that smile hiding a sad person? What about the women who work in the stores?

I still wonder about my parents. Has it made them happy to do everything they've done for Ron, Karen, and me? Is Karen happy at school in Boston? She doesn't have time to skate as much as she used to. Is she happy pursuing other things?

Am *I* happy? Is it possible to be happy without skating?

My dad says that the thing that makes me happiest has nothing at all to do with skating. He says it's *giving*.

Once or twice a year, I take three humongous bags filled with stuffed animals to the children's hospital. These are the stuffed animals that fans give me all year long. That really does make me happy — just to see those kids smile for a minute.

I'm also a national spokesperson for the Children's Miracle Network. I co-chair the Pro-Kids program with Bo Jackson. One of the things I do is co-host their telethon. Spending time with Bo and with Steven Young and

Mary Lou Retton, who are also involved, is so much fun that it doesn't seem like work at all. Most of all I love being around kids, and the time flies when I'm with them or doing something to help them.

My father has always told me that my love for skating has to come from me and only me. He says if I stop feeling that passion I should stop skating. So I'm always asking myself whether I'm truly happy doing what I'm doing, whether it's truly what I want.

That's why it's so important for me to try all kinds of different things, and compare them to skating. But I've always found that skating is closest to my heart.

22

Dad's List

One day, at the beginning of the 1995–96 season, I asked my dad to tell me what my weaknesses were. This was a kind of family tradition. He'd just given Ron and Karen a list of their shortcomings that they needed to fix. We're all used to that kind of honesty from him. But he hadn't said anything to me for a while.

Dad thought about my question for two days. Then he shrugged and said, "I can't think of anything."

Hmm. Of course I liked the answer then, but a year later I knew that his answer wouldn't be the same. As the 1996-97 season was gearing up, I just didn't feel like myself. Lots of things had been going wrong. Karen was gone and I missed her. After the tour, after losing

Harris, I had a hard time adjusting to being home.

Practice wasn't going so well, either. My new skates were a nightmare. Dad made the heels lower, then higher. The blades were messed up, too. When I wanted to go one way, they'd go the other. We were spending hours a day working on my new program, and my feet were killing me.

I was not happy.

So I went back, and I said, "Dad, can you please tell me what my problems are now?"

Well, this time he didn't even have to think. He came up with so many answers that I needed a pen and paper to write them down. I almost wanted to say, "Sorry I asked."

First on his list was *appreciation*. Dad said I needed to appreciate my life more.

What did he mean? Appreciate my gold medals? Appreciate my talent? Appreciate *him*? "Everything," he said. Everything!

The next thing on Dad's list was *perspective*. I had lost my perspective on the sport. Where did it fit into the *big* picture of my life — the picture of me, not only as a skater, but as a *person*? Had I forgotten that skating wasn't all of life?

Throughout the year, the list kept growing. I

knew he was right, but I didn't know how to fix my problems. And he couldn't tell me. No one could. The only solution I could come up with was *work*. So, I buckled down and worked harder than ever.

I tried to remember my motto. Have fun, Michelle, I told myself, have *fun*! But I was forcing it. Karen wasn't around to help me laugh at myself. I began to realize that a motto gives you something to reach for, but it doesn't count for much if you can't put it into action.

I started talking to myself — not out loud but in my head. Even after the beginning of the season went well and I had won a couple of competitions, there were these two nagging voices in my head.

One voice — the bad voice — would say, "You're going to fall. Everybody's got to fall sometime." And the other voice would say, "Shut up. Don't listen to that, Michelle!"

I went back to the rink and practiced my jumps. I tried to shut out the bad voice. But I kept on having second thoughts on the ice. It was the first time this had happened to me in skating.

In the days leading up to the 1997 Nationals in Nashville, Tennessee, reporters asked me how I was dealing with the pressure of being a defending champion. I'd won six gold medals since San Jose. People were saying I couldn't be beat. How did I do it? they asked.

I thought about my motto and the things my mom and dad had always told me. I purposely *didn't* think about the bad voice I'd been hearing. I told those reporters, with a big smile, "Well, I try to go out there and have fun. I try to remember that it's just a sport. It isn't everything. It's fun." That's just about what I said . . . on national television in front of millions of people.

Then I skated. My short program went well, and I was in first place going into the freeskate. But very few people saw the short program on TV. Millions, on the other hand, saw the freeskate.

That's when it happened. I fell once, then again, and then again. . . . Aaugh! I won't go over it all again.

My dad was right. I had lost perspective. I wasn't skating for the reason I always had — to have fun and fly free. Instead, I was skating not to lose. How had I done this? How had I let the anticipation of this night — this one competition — grow and grow out of proportion, all year long? That wasn't like me at all.

131

After my program, the world did not see a girl who had just had fun. They saw a girl who was weeping. And this time, not from joy. I was confused and mad at myself, and so disappointed.

Afterward, the reporters wanted to know why it happened. Was it the pressure? Some speculated that it was partly because my body had changed. They said that as it had matured, my balance had been affected, and I couldn't do the jumps with my usual ease.

It's true I had changed. I hadn't looked at a single tape of myself all year until after Nationals. When I finally did, I hardly recognized myself. Yes, I looked older. But it wasn't my body that looked different — my big growth spurt had happened the year before. It was something in my eye, something inside me. I just looked *off*.

Regardless of how serious the role of Salome was, the part of me that was young and hopeful always shone through when I skated it. I think it did, anyway. I knew then that skating was just a sport and that it wasn't everything.

All of these things confirmed what I knew that night in Nashville. I knew the answer right away when my dad asked me, "Well, Michelle, what did you learn from this?"

It all clicked into place. I learned that I needed to love the sport again. That's what my dad meant by appreciation and perspective. I needed to love skating for what it was.

I needed to get back to the feeling I'd had before I was world champion. In a way, I needed to become that little kid I'd left behind in Birmingham again. The kid who didn't win any medals at all, but who felt like she had it all. Because she could really *skate*.

23

Getting Up Again

After the 1997 Nationals, lots of people were supportive of me and worried about me in the nicest way. They knew that Worlds was coming up, and it seemed like they wanted to protect me.

A few days after Nationals, Brian Boitano called. He was the first skater to check up on me. "Are you doing okay?" he asked. I told him I was fine. He said, "I hate to be a cliché, but you always learn *something* from bad experiences. What did you learn?"

I didn't know where to begin. I was still sorting it all out. But Brian told me that he could see the panic in my face. He could tell that I had been thinking negative thoughts. And he gave me some great advice.

He said that I shouldn't approach each jump thinking about what could go wrong — What if I lean too far forward? What if I don't have enough speed? Instead, I should *see* the good, clean, upright landing. As I'm speeding into a jump, I should say instead, "All I have to do is stand up straight."

He was right. That negative voice in my head had been blasting. I had thought I could just ignore it, but somehow that had only made it louder.

Frank said I needed to attack. I couldn't hold myself back anymore. I had to let myself go free and skate like I love to skate. He was right, too.

Everyone was right. Sometimes the biggest test of a skater or any athlete is the moment after she falls. Can she find the spirit and the guts to get up and go on? I planned to do all those things in March at the Worlds in Lausanne, Switzerland. I wouldn't be afraid. I would try to skate free.

The media in Lausanne had set up the competition as a duel between Tara Lipinski and me. I was the veteran (at sixteen!), the "artistic" skater. Tara was the wonder kid, the amazing jumping bean who couldn't fall. She was the "technical" skater.

But all skaters know that you have to be strong in both areas if you want to be a champion. And I for one had to compete with myself before I could even think about Tara.

I went into the short program with the highest hopes and the most positive attitude I could. I did fine . . . until I stepped out on one jump and stumbled on the landing.

I was so mad at myself when it was over. I was crying already. I started picturing myself in my long program — falling just as I had at Nationals.

But in the middle of Worlds, a couple of *really* terrible things happened that made my problems seem minuscule. Carlo Fassi, one of the most famous coaches in all of skating, passed away in Lausanne. He had coached Peggy Fleming and Dorothy Hamill and so many others. He'd been working with Nicole Bobek all year at Ice Castle. I'd seen him every day.

He died suddenly. Everyone was shocked. Amazingly, his wife, Christa, held herself together and helped Nicole get through the competition.

Then, Scott Hamilton, one of the best and biggest-hearted skaters of all time, announced that he had cancer. It's a type of cancer that has a high rate of recovery, and he assured everyone that he would be okay. But compared to that, my triple Lutz seemed about as terrible as a pimple.

After the short program, I was sitting in the locker room changing into my street shoes. I thought about Carlo and his family. I thought about Scott. While I was thinking so hard, I yanked on my shoelaces, and one of them snapped. My hand flew back and smacked me in the face.

Suddenly I started laughing. I *needed* that whack in the head. What had I been thinking? Skating isn't a matter of life and death.

The former world champion Lu Chen, had finished twenty-fifth after the short program and didn't even qualify for the freeskate. She'd had real problems all year. But I was fourth. I still had a shot. What's more, I was at my favorite competition, Worlds.

Just after that, Frank told me that an old man had grabbed his arm and said, "Go tell Michelle that she's the best skater in the world." I laughed some more. With all this support, how could I lose?

I skated second to last in the long program. I

137

glided out to the middle of the rink and took my opening pose. I knew that people were already holding their breath, wondering if I would fall apart like at Nationals.

Karen was home in Boston, and I knew that she was holding her breath, too. She'd made me promise that I'd call her as soon as I got off the ice, even though it would be four in the morning her time. Mom and Dad were holding their breath, too, there in the stands, watching.

But I wasn't going to fall. I was going to fly. The music started, and I skated. I dug down deep and took off. As I stroked the ice, moving faster and faster, I felt that wonderful breeze in my face. All around me the arena was sparkling. The crowd was behind me. I wasn't afraid. Yes, skating was just a sport, but a great sport. I know Scott Hamilton and Carlo Fassi would agree.

I made one small mistake, where I turned a triple into a double. But I kept telling myself, like Brian said, Just stand up straight and everything will be fine. And it was. Every jump was clean. Every spin was centered.

When it was over, although I'd won the freeskate, my mistake in the short program had cost me. Tara won, and I came in second overall. But that was fine. My wings were back. Not a single tear fell. Some people said I was the happiest silver medalist they'd ever seen. I think they were right.

24

Taking Off

My plan for this year, with the Olympics coming up, is to work hard, be myself, and have as much fun as I possibly can. Anyone who works hard enough deserves to win the Olympics. I want to deserve to win.

This year I want to skate for myself. I don't want to think about any other skater. I just want to think about the thing I love to do most. Who knows how much longer I'll do it? I want to appreciate it now while it's happening.

I also want to get back that feeling I've always had about skating. It's the feeling I get when I step on the ice and I'm in control. I sense everything that's going on around me, and it feels completely natural. That's when I can let myself fly.

My program this year is very different from

my past programs. What I love most about it is its spirit. The music is really *me*. It's kind of romantic, with a feeling of yearning in it. It reminds me of how I feel about the future. Not just the Olympics, but the whole big future ahead of me. Do you know this feeling? It's a feeling of wanting something so much, but you don't know exactly what it is? That's what I'm talking about.

When I became world champion in 1996, everything started happening so fast that I almost couldn't appreciate how lucky and how happy I was. I wished then that I could take a picture of my life so I could look at it at the same time that I was living it.

Sometimes parents of other skaters go to my mom and dad for advice. They want to know how they can keep their kids' childhood from slipping away. My parents try to explain how Karen and I did it. Even though we put our hearts into skating, we always reserved a special place for the other parts of our lives. And they always tell those parents that the hardest thing was helping us to keep our *happiness* from slipping away.

When I look at the kids training today at Ice Castle I can tell which ones are going to do well. It's not necessarily the ones who have the most natural talent or who fall the least. Sometimes it's the kids who fall the *most,* and keep pulling themselves up and trying again. They're the ones I admire. They're the ones with *heart.*

The kids who'll do best are the ones who are in their skates waiting for their turn on the ice. Their parents don't have to nag them to practice or push them onto the rink. They're ready. "Let's go!" they say.

I was one of those kids. If you saw me when I was little, you wouldn't have thought I was anything special. If I had a "spark," like some people say I did, it wasn't the way I jumped or spun. It was a spark in my heart. I was always so happy to be on the ice. If I fell, I put it out of my mind and got back to the thing I loved to do.

I've fallen so many times in my life! But I've always gotten up again. As a result, maybe I've accomplished more than most kids my age. But the fact is that I'm still just seventeen — and seventeen is *seventeen,* no matter how many gold medals I have. My future is as much a mystery as any other teenager's. I feel kind of scared and kind of excited about it, at the same time.

Like most people, my future can't be neatly mapped out. My mom and dad always tell me that there are many roads ahead to choose from. You can pick one, but you can never be sure where it will lead. It may branch out at some point and go in another direction you didn't foresee.

There's good and bad along every road and in every life, they say. But if you can just try to appreciate the good when it's happening, instead of after it's gone, maybe it'll be a little easier to get through the bad. I think it's true that the hardest part of being an athlete — of being a person — is grabbing hold of the moment and *appreciating* it, like my parents always say.

This book is a kind of picture of my life and all those moments I wish I'd been able to capture and hold. The growing up. The falling down. The getting up. The competing. The losing. The winning. Put them in any order you like. They're all a part of who I am.

I can appreciate all of my experiences now, looking back on them. But as they were happening, did I really *feel* my life? Right now, I want to keep my eyes and my heart open, so that my new experiences don't pass me by.

143

I know that my life will never be *all* good or *all* bad. But if I'm lucky, I'll have more good than bad.

And if I'm very lucky, I'll *know* it.

Glossary

Here's a glossary of moves. Jumps and spins sound pretty fun and simple on paper but, believe me, it took lots and lots of lessons and practice for me to be able to do them. Never try a new skill without a teacher to help you.

Axel jump: You take off from one foot, going forward, spin at least one and a half times in the air, and land on the other foot, going backward. In a *waltz jump*, which is sort of an Axel for beginners, you do a half revolution in the air before you land. Most of the top women skaters do a double Axel, which is two and a half revolutions. (The rest of the jumps I'll tell you about are simpler to explain: a single means one revolution, a double means two revolutions, etc.) Most of the top-level men can do triple Axels, but so far only Midori Ito and Tonya Harding have landed one in women's competition. It takes really strong thigh muscles.

Butterfly: Skaters usually save butterflies for the ends of their programs because they're real crowd pleasers and make a big finish. It really does look like a butterfly. The skater's body rotates in a horizontal position over the ice while her legs whirl in the air behind her. The hardest thing about it is that you can't see where you're going.

Camel Spin: A funny name for a beautiful spin! This one is done in an arabesque (that's a ballet word) position, with one leg straight out behind you, parallel to the ice. I guess they call it a "camel" because beginners look humpy when they first try to do one. When you do a big jump into this spin it's called a *flying camel.*

Combination: Two jumps in a row. As soon as you land the first jump, you have to take off into the second jump. To do one triple jump, you need to build up a lot of speed on your entry into the jump. To do two in a row, you need even more speed!

Edges: Each blade on a pair of skates has two edges — an inside edge and an outside edge. Once a beginning skater has learned how to stand up straight on the ice, she learns how to lean into her edges. It's scary at first, but great skating means not being afraid to use your edges. Watch a skater's edges when she skates forward or backward, when she takes off into a jump, and when she's gliding across the ice in a spiral.

Flip jump: One of the hardest jumps. First you do a little turn on the ice (a "three-turn" or a "mohawk"). Then you dig one toe pick into the ice behind you and use it to push yourself into the air, like a pole vaulter. You take off of a back inside edge, spin at least once in the air, and land on the picking foot. People sometimes confuse this jump with the back flips that gymnasts do, but it's completely different. Top-level skaters do triple flips.

Footwork: One of the requirements in both the long and the short program is a series of fast connected steps. The judges watch closely to make sure footwork is fast and clean — not sloppy — and that the skater is covering the full surface of the ice.

Jump: I'm sure you know what a jump is, but judges look for other things in a jump besides a clean landing. They want to see good speed going into the jump and good speed coming out of it. Jumps should be high in the air and cover a great distance. The body should be held straight and tight when it's spinning up there. The landing should be on one foot, not two.

Kiss and Cry: What skaters call the area where they wait with their coaches for their scores to come up. Sometimes you kiss, sometimes you cry. Sometimes you do both.

Layback spin: You spin on one foot and lean back from the waist while your "free" leg (the one you're not spinning on) and your arms are in pretty positions. The lower you can bend backward, the better the judges like it. Practicing this over and over again kills your back!

Long program: Also called the "freeskate." For women, four minutes. For men, four and a half minutes. It is the most important part of a competition and the place where artistry counts the most.

Loop jump: This jump starts from a back outside edge and lands on the same back outside edge. If you use a toe pick to get you into the air, it's called a *toe-loop*.

Lutz jump: This is like a loop except that you take off on one foot and land on the *other* one.

Marks: Each of the judges gives two sets of marks to each skater, in both the long and the short programs — one set for technical requirements and the other for artistic expression. A score of 6.0 (the highest mark possible) means the judge thought the skater was perfect.

Salchow (*sal*-kow) jump: A jump that takes off of one back inside edge and lands on the back outside edge of the other foot. This one's easy to spot because you'll see the skater do a little one-foot turn on the ice at the beginning of it.

Short program: Also called the "technical program." Two minutes and thirty seconds long. In the short program, the skater does eight required elements in any order she chooses.

Spin: There are lots of different kinds of spins — sit spins, scratch spins, camel spins, laybacks, etc. In the short program, each spin has to have at least eight revolutions; in the long program, at least six. The rules say that there have to be *combinations* of spins, too, which means you have to change feet and position without slowing down your spin. Watch to see if a spin is fast and centered on one little spot on the ice — the judges do.

Spiral: A spiral shows off lots of things, especially speed, flexibility, and edge quality. You extend one leg behind you, as high as you can make it go, then you glide across the ice with all your weight on one edge of your skate. I do an inside/outside spiral in my new program. I start my spiral at one end of the rink and do a giant *S* all the way to the other end, shifting from an inside to an outside edge as I go.

Split jump: This is a flashy move. You jump into the air in a split position and touch your ankle or your toe with your hand.

Spread eagle: With your two heels facing each other and your toes pointed straight out, you glide in an arc around the ice.

Toe-loop jump (see "Loop jump" for details): Some of the top men skaters can do *quadruple* toe-loops!

Toe pick: The teeth on the front of the figure skate blade. (Hockey and speed skates don't have them.) Skaters use their toe picks in lots of jumps and spins, and they're a big help. But they also leave holes in the ice. Sometimes you hit someone else's hole when you're doing a jump. It's scary at first, but we all practice how to recover when that happens.

Zamboni: The big machine that makes the ice smooth. A lot of people think the ice looks slippery after the Zamboni has cleaned it, but it's not. I love perfectly smooth ice with no holes or scratches in it. Very good for flying. . . .